DEAD MOUSE

AND OTHER MISTEAKS

COUNTRY POETRY

BY

D. W. MAILAND

Illustrated by D.W. Mailand

There once was a Montana clown
who found stories in country and town.
When his ~~friends~~ ran amok
He'd record their bad luck
Though they warned him,
"Now don't write that down!"

D.W. Mailand

Wordclay
1663 Liberty Drive, Suite 200
Bloomington, IN 47403
www.wordclay.com

First published by Wordclay on 3/12/2009.

ISBN 978-1-6048-1498-9 (sc)

Printed in the United States of America.

This book is printed on acid-free paper.

DEDICATION

This effort is dedicated to the memory of my mother,
Frieda Anna Lisbet Daleske Mailand, my biggest fan.
When I sent her a sample of my writing, she didn't
respond at all. By and by, when my wife called to ask
how she had enjoyed the poems, she said, "Well, I can't figure
out why he spends all that time writing poetry. His brother will
be here next week. I'll let him read them." In her own words:
"Ninety-three years old; what can you expect?"

ACKNOWLEDGEMENTS

More than anybody else I can think of, the Eides ... Les, Jackie and Matt ... of the Sweetgrass Hills are responsible for this book. Matt, one of the most reluctant cowboy poets in Montana, has contributed a number of notable efforts, and has inspired me to try "real hard" to do it right. The Montana Country Poets and Pickers of Havre, MT ... Arnold and "Sug" Hokanson, Dave Molitor, Jim Faber, Fred Liese, S.R. Hughes, Dusty Huestis, Rick Johnston, Ron Pegar, Doug White ... were instrumental in providing coaching, as well as a forum for my efforts. Bonnie Williamson and the staff at Havre/Hill County Library, and Becky Ross and members of the Havre Art Association furnished many opportunities to meet the public. My fellow Harlemites and other area residents deserve many thanks for being so "poem-o-genic". And finally, my family ... Loxi, Marisa and Damon ... showed a great deal of patience and courage in reading my stuff and bragging about it now and then. Their criticisms were always constructive, I think.

CONTENTS

CHAPTER 1 - MOSTLY WIMMEN

CHAPTER 2 : HOME ON THE RANGE

CHAPTER 3 : THE WILD COUNTRYSIDE

CHAPTER 4: SMORGASBORD

CHAPTER 5 : POETS AND PICKERS

INTRODUCTION

I have been a writer for many years. I was copywriter for KDIX radio and TV in Dickinson, ND. Then I moved to Montana and worked as copywriter for KOJM in Havre. Graduating from NoMoCo with an English/History major, I taught high school English at Harlem. To that point, I was writing for profit ... I got a paycheck for writing. Then I began writing country poetry. That took care of the "writing-for-pay" idea, pretty much. Without a market for my efforts, I needed SOME kind of feedback. I began to participate in Cowboy Poetry Gatherings. The response of the audience became my "paycheck"!

While I married a Montana ranch girl and the in-laws furnish some pretty lively stories, much of my poetry is about people other than cowboys. Most are just plain country folk. (True, some are quite unusual and quirky.) But they all have one thing in common: the spirit of the West. These are hard-working, hard-playing folks who stand on their own feet, independent and resourceful, not afraid to tackle something new, and blessed with a strong sense of humor and justice.

DEAD MOUSE

and

OTHER MISTEAKS

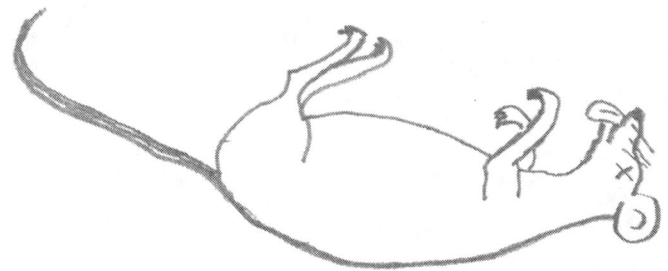

CHAPTER ONE

MOSTLY WIMMEN

*　　*　　*　　*　　*

Because men and women perceive life differently, the contrast provides for endless fascination and entertainment.

BAKIN' FOOL

We have a friend who loves to cook but doesn't like to doodle.
It raised some eyebrows when she came to supper with a strudel.
The crust, a gossamer delight, she hand-placed every flake.
With luscious fruity blend inside, she got a perfect bake.
She wrapped it gently for the trip with parchment underneath.
It was too fine to violate with knife and fork and teeth.
We served a slice to everyone, with ice cream on the side.
Our glowing comments should have filled
      the baker's heart with pride.
Utensils poised and tastebuds set, our lips began to smack.
Our baker took one teeny bite and promptly uttered ,
         "ACK !"
"You uttered 'Ack !'" the hostess cried.
 "What ails you now, fair baker?
We scarce expected such a word …
 not from our strudelmaker !"
"I hate cranberries ! Raisins, too !
 I cringe with every bite !
I should have used some other fruit
to make this strudel right!"
"Pray tell, dear baker, why on earth
you used this combination ?"
"I used it in the interest
of resource conservation !
I ate the other fruits contained in Costco's dried fruit mix.
I baked this strudel just to save me from a wasteful fix !"
"Then, why did you accept a slice, and even take a bite ?"
"I had to sample what I brought you, just to be polite !"
She never ate the strudel and we knew she never would.
We learned : some bakers bake because… because …
      To Bake Is Good !

This driver still insists she saw, in her peripheral vision,
the bird rise beside the passenger door, fly forward,
and smash her mirror .

BIRD BLUES

There are lots of folks familiar with
            how quick our friend can drive.
With "The Limit", her velocity
            stays down near seventy-five.
But one Friday, it's the truth, so help me,
            may they strike me blind,
Her misfortune was to meet
            "The Grouse that Struck Her from Behind".

This was not the first bird hit by her ;
            she took a pheasant, too,
And her Taurus headlight cost two-fifty
            when repairs were through,
So on more than one occasion she expressed
            her sharp-tongued ire
Wishing that late chicken from the frying pan
            to Brimstone Fire .

In the interim, she turned to hocus-pocus
            when she drove,
Telling creatures on the roadside just to stay there …
            not to move,
And it worked for quite a while
            until her magic spells grew lax,
But of course, one can't prepare
            for rear-assaulting bird attacks.

It is odd this superstitious gal
            ignored an omen clear.
Just two days before, she left
            the highschool parking lot, no fear,
And a student tossed his apple at her car,
            and hit it, too !
"None so blind as will not see" …
            there's not a lot a friend can do.

So the Friday of the incident,
        three gals were shopping-bound.
All attention was on what's ahead …
        who thinks to turn around ?
They're approaching Zurich.
        Fiendish fowl at roadside lay in wait
Wryly smiling, heart and mind a-boil
        with car-and-driver hate.

When the car sped by, the bird leaped up
        and made its fowl attack,
Rose BESIDE the door, flew FORWARD,
        gave the mirror quite a whack.
Driver saw the puff of feathers,
        said some words and sped along.
Then the passenger remarked,
        "The rearview mirror glass is gone !"

Now we mourn the passing
        of the world's first supersonic grouse,
And our friend prepares for car bills
        with a mortgage on her house,
And she warns : Avoid misfortune
        that can cause you lots of flack.
When you pass a roadside bird, get set, look sharp,
        and watch your back !

FOUR WHEEL HAZARD

You couldn't say she's the most ferocious shopper
   in the aisle
Although there's focus and a fierce resolve
   behind her smile.
Her years as nurse and teacher put that firm tone
   in her voice
So when she speaks, things happen ; no one needs
   to ask her twice.
She doesn't mean to be abrupt,
   but when stuff "just won't go",
She loses patience quickly and her "safety valve"
   will blow.
And though she feels regret, most times,
   it's too hard to explain
So, whether right or wrong,
   that first impression will remain.

One time, her little girl "came with"
   to help her grocery shop
By hanging from the cart,
   though mom had often told her, "Stop !"
So when, once more,
   the urchin's calisthenics did not quit,
While turning from Aisle One,
   mom felt compelled to holler, "Git!"
And instantly, in Aisle Two,
   some nice lady spun around
And quickly scooted right back up
   the aisle she'd just come down !

It doesn't happen every time ;
   some shopping trips are tame,
But even when she's clearly wrong,
   she doesn't get the blame !
Why, just last week while rolling up the aisle
   to buy some meat,
She gawked to left and right
   her "cart control" quite indiscreet.
A man was bending over,
   searching for the perfect chop.

She rammed him in the bum ;
　　　　he took a nasty belly-flop.
But did he call her to account
　　　　or have harsh words to say ?
No ! He apologized at length
　　　　for standing in her way !

I feel an obligation
　　　　to advise you where she'll be
But she's gone to Hawaii, Minot,
　　　　Whitefish, Calgary.
She shopped Thermopolis
　　　　and Rapid City, Lewistown,
Great Falls and Billings,
　　　　so you see, she really moves around.
I'd name her and describe her,
　　　　but that's probably too late
For, once you run across her,
　　　　you're a victim of your fate.
And often, nothing happens
　　　　and she's just as nice as pie !
Meanwhile, watch who's approaching
　　　　from the corner of your eye.

GET ME OUTTA HERE !

There are lots of things in Harlem never happen any more
And a lot of things in Harlem never happened once before
And a bunch of things in Harlem likely never come again
But we don't expect them happening from preacher-lady Jane.

On a snowy Wednesday afternoon at quarter after three
At the Bardanouve Post Office, ably manned by Jan and me,
Suddenly she entered, anxious, as if humped against the cold,
Not impeccable as usual, but somewhat uncontrolled.

Ordinarily, she bubbles with enthusiastic glee.
Not this time ! She came for help, for she was growing panicky
With the look of coyote-in-a-trap or deer-in-headlight-glare
And decidedly disheveled, squirming, fretting, waiting there.

Like a snake about to change its skin, or butterfly, emerge,
She hiked up her long blue eider coat and gave a mighty surge.
"Oh ! I can't get out ! My zipper's stuck !
          Do something if you can !"
(Such a one is best assisted by a woman, not a man.)

And with little muss or fuss,
          Jan's practiced fingers made the save
And the hiked-up layers settled back with every tug she gave
And our preacher-lady's dignity survived the crisis mode
And I thanked my lucky stars that I was spared this heavy load.

There are lots of things in Harlem never happen any more
And a lot of things in Harlem never happened once before
And a bunch of things in Harlem likely never come again
Like the rescue of our slightly claustrophobic preacher, Jane.

GOOD THINKIN'

My missus ain't no slouch at planning 'way ahead, I think.
She lets the dirty dishes pile up all day in the sink.
We sure ain't short of dishes ;
there's lots more where they come from,
So washing every meal wastes time ;
 in fact, she says, it's dumb.

Well, I do lots of oddball jobs that can be sorta dirty
And, bein' fussy, like to give 'em back cleaned up real purty.
And at our house there's only one big sink …
 it's in the kitchen …
So, when I haul in all my stuff, there's bound to be some … complaining.

By then, she's got a customer, or talkin' on the phone.
I tell myself at such a time, "My boy, you're on your own."
No apron, so I often splash bleach water on my crotch.
It's just as well there's no one here to supervise …
         or watch.

But I must quickly clear the sink to get on with my life.
I bow my head domestically, a substitute housewife.
And when I'm done, she ambles in
and gives the mildest screech ;
 "I love the smell of hot soap water
mixed with Clorox bleach !"

"I believe I'll give the neighbors Christmas presents
        warm and toasty.
Every time their face AIN'T freezin' off,
        they'll think of me and smile.
And, I think I'll sew 'em up myself.
        Not bein' proud or boasty,
But, if wife can sew, then I should catch on
        in a little while !"

So he hit the fabric store for polar fleece ...
        who cares what color ?
For a "necker" or a "gator", it's the function,
        not the style.
And with that, this big, tough, rugged outdoor
        horse-and-cowboy feller
Headed for the sewing room with swagger,
        confidence and smile.
Was it faith or flair, beginner's luck,
        good sense or concentration ?
This rough seamster never heard of french,
        flat fell, zig-zag or serge.
Sewing back and forth about ten times
        with grim determination
He completed six neckwarmer gifts
        to satisfy his urge.

"Hey there, Missus ! Where's your Quick Stitch ?
        I still have to do some patchin'
On my coveralls. That one-hand rig
        should do the job just right !"
But the missus loved her Quick Stitch.
        She'd been thinkin' and a-watchin'.
He won't get a chance to wreck that handy tool
        without a fight !
Okie-Doke ! The big machine would likely do the job
        much neater.
Full of pride, success and confidence,
        he tackled his next job.
Hacked a denim kneepatch off old Levis ...
        (how could life be sweeter ?)

Patch those costly insulated coveralls
      and save a gob !

Evidently, this machine was not
      a denim/canvas sewer
For it "powered-out" before the patching job
      was well-begun.
If he found the "Power" knob,
      (it should be labeled "Higher/Lower"),
He could crank it up for heavy stuff
      and make his final run.

Every cowboy knows the basic principles
      of motivation :
On a tractor, shove the throttle up
      or shift to lower gear.
On a horse, a touch of rein or spur
      provides such inspiration.
When you're finished, throttle back
      or holler "Whoa !"…so what's to fear?
So he twisted knobs and dials and levers,
      feeling light and breezy.
Then the thread broke two, three times.
      His big hands strung it up again.
In the field, when baler twine got busted,
      he could fix it easy.
A familiar job, re-stringing .
      This should be about the same.

The machine, of course, was down-and-out.
      He called his chief mechanic.
She surveyed the wreck and wondered
      if she'd have to make him dead.
Carefully, she read the handbook,
      striving bravely not to panic.
Half an hour she vainly fiddled,
      and what spicy words she said !

Then he told about re-stringing …
      like the baler, only smaller.
"Did you touch the bobbin tension ?"
      "Give 'er here. I'll snug 'er down !"

"NEVER MIND !" She fixed his threading mess;
    her face was flushed with color.
Thankfully, the kids weren't there.
        Her BEST expression was a frown.

So, our cowboy learned that baling
        is not quite the same as mending ...
Banned from sewing on the console
        and the Quick Stitch tool as well.
She's the only seamstress now.
        He carefully avoids offending.
Still ... a heavy-duty Power-Stitch machine
        would sure be swell !

INDISPENSABLE

There still is one thing I can do for my wife.
It's a chore she has begged me to do all our life.
Such a manly endeavor, stout-hearted and brave,
Which is something I do with a nonchalant wave.
It is not honing knives ; she can use them quite dull
And she empties the ash pan whenever it's full.
She will fetch in some kindling to keep our house warm.
When our houseguests arrive, she can turn on the charm.
She has juggled kids, housekeeping, church,
        school and work ...
(I can tell you, this lady is not one to shirk .)
But one job, so abhorrent, she recoils in fright
(And it might be what makes her wake up in the night .)
One predictable panic ... unwarranted fear ...
(Possibly, the one reason she lets me live here .)
She entreats me so meekly, my heart fills with pride
And I think, 'She's so lucky I stand by her side !'
Then she hands me that awful device to prepare
And she leaves the room ; this job she'd rather not share.
In my strong hands I grab the projecting pull strip
And I spiral it down with a sneer on my lip.
Then I press on the cardboard right where it says "Squeeze"
And the whole can explodes with a BANG and a breeze !
Then she gratefully gives me a look full of lovin'
And pops ready-to-bake biscuits into our oven.

Every May, oversize and overweight envelopes arrive at the Post Office, and the mothers, bless their hearts, always pay the extra tariff.

MOTHER'S DAY GREETINGS

Hi Mom ! I hope you got the card ... the biggest one they had.
I knew the fancy lace and tune
       would make your old heart glad.
I mailed it just past closing time and couldn't get it weighed.
I took a chance and sent it so it wouldn't be delayed.
The pictures might have bulked it up an extra ounce or two.
I hope you don't mind greetings and good wishes
       "Postage Due".

*   *   *   *   *   *   *

HOT AIR HASSLE

There's a basic conflict raging at the bedrock of my home.
It's a turmoil that has boiled near forty years.
It's a summer disagreement that invades our comfort zone
And it renders both combatants close to tears.
It's a fight based on the placement of the old electric fan .
(That's like "central air for dinosaurs", you know.)
Just a step above the open window letting in the breeze
But it works BOTH days Montana winds don't blow.

Even imitation wind will help to make warm air feel cool
So, no argument ... electric fans are great.
When you have to sit indoors and work,
       a flow of air feels good.
But it's OVERNIGHT fan placement we debate.

Now, it's her rock-hard opinion,
        fans are made for blowing air
And you set them up the same way, day or night.
At the open door or window,
        all those blades must push air IN.
(She'll get up to check if I have turned it right !)

My idea : a house with hot air needs some way
        to pull it OUT.
It's a plan for overnight I aim to keep.
When I set up my exhaust fan at the far end of the house,
Gentle fresh air fills the bedroom where we sleep.

Well ! At last we got 'er figured how both sides
        can prove they're right.
Now we EACH have fans to push and pull our air
And, although they neutralize each other,
        all the fighting's done …
A solution both of us consider fair.

So we swelter in our stalemate ; neither one has given in
And we get on better than we thought we could.
But we're glad we're in Montana
where the zephyrs MOSTLY blow,
And on nights like THAT … we ventilate real good !

THE JOY OF SOUP

How do you handle a bucket of soup
    Free, creamy hot soup
    Good mushroomy soup ?
What do you do with three gallons of soup
At nine o'clock Tuesday evening ?

Get smaller buckets and pour in your soup
    One gallon of soup
    Two gallons of soup
Old ice cream buckets are handy for soup
To store awhile in your cooler.

How do you carry three gallons of soup
    Full buckets of soup
    Fresh, steamy hot soup ?
You have to be careful transporting your soup
All the way to your cooler.

Stack up and cuddle your buckets of soup
    One gallon on top
    Two gallons below.
You maybe can carry a tower of soup
Across the street to your cooler.

A hot plastic lid can't support that much soup …
    Eight pounds to the gallon
    Or just a bit more.
You're bound for a wreck with a tower of soup
Before you pass over the carpet !

Oh, No ! Something's wrong with my tower of soup …
  Fresh, sticky hot soup
  Three gallons of soup !
The lid will not hold up a gallon of soup !
My tower is slowly collapsing !

My tower has turned to a fountain of soup
  A gusher of soup
  A carpet of soup !
Archimedes could figure the volume of soup
When one bucket sinks into another !

I'll save what is left of my mushroomy soup
  About half my soup
  Lip-smackin' good soup.
Bernoulli should study my tower of soup
To check his old hydraulic theory !

LOOK! UP IN THE SKY!
IT'S A BIRD! IT'S A PLANE!
IT'S A SEWER SNAKE!

You can't convince Vince till he sees for himself;
    On some subjects, he's sure that he's right.
        When he's doing "men's work" and his missus butts in
          It's potentially time for a fight.
When their sewer got clogged, Vince rented a snake …
    (Roto-Rooter that plugs in the wall.)
        With the right tool, the knowledge, the need and the will
          He would clear it in no time at all !
At the basement cleanout, he fed in the snake.
    There's resistance, and often, delay.
        When you can't see your target, it's "progress by faith";
          One must hope that one heads the right way.
As the project dragged on, Debbie mentioned the noise
    Like a rattle and scrape in the wall.
        By and by, it seemed higher … now louder upstairs.
          (Debbie IS his helpmate, after all.)
But he scoffed at her weak understanding of sound …
    How it telegraphs all points at once
        And might seem to be coming from here or from there
          As we all know … (unless we're a dunce .)
After much extreme effort … two hours and a half …
    He did not seem much further ahead.
        It was time for a break so he wandered outdoors
          And he saw where his snake had been fed.
Sticking out of the air vent on top of the roof
    Roughly six feet of snake gently waved,
        But I doubt that he ranted or cussed at the waste ;
          (Vince has always been quite well-behaved.)
With no further delay, Vince untangled the snake,
    Cleared the drain clog and "that's all she wrote".
        But for lending support when she knew he was wrong,
          I guess Debbie's entitled to gloat.

MELON SEASON

Now, your next-of-kin are not the folks you really want to tell on
If you'd rather just continue with a peaceful, happy life
But in case you catch one at her desk and thumping on her melon,
Then the average husband stops and re-evaluates his wife.

Just the other day I stopped to give a howdy to my missus.
She was pulling hair on left and right and thumping on her head.
I was too surprised to jump right in with cuddles, hugs and kisses
And her look of concentration was enough to stop me dead.

"Do you think my head should still be numb from visiting
        the doctor ?
If my ear is back to normal, should my head be normal too ?"
It was not a time for jokes or any words that might have
        shocked her
So I said, I didn't know. It was the most that I could do.

I have seen such thumping, pulling, squeezing, probing
        concentration
At the grocer's fruit and veggie shelf, in spite of all the signs.
They will mumble "Green !" or "Rotten !", or accepting
        approbation,
But for thumping heads, there simply are not any standard lines.

I believe I muttered something nice to calm and reassure her
And to buy some time until the numbness dissipates away.
But if YOUR wife thumps her melon, don't play hero
        just to cure her.
Smile, and nod, and walk away … and have an ordinary day !

Spheksophobia = Fear of Wasps

Our family has long recognized a "difference" between East and West Montana. We have some Westside relatives. If you are a Westsider, we're sorry.

LOWDOWN BUZZIN' BLUES

My sis-in-law has likes and hates, which everybody does.
I think her biggest hate is for the bugs that sting and buzz.
It's not the honey-making kind, or ones that pollinate.
It's not the bumble-buzzing kind that hardly aggravate.
It's not the sweat bee or leaf roller, teeny flies that vex.
It's Yellow Jackets she considers "Bee-O-Saurus Rex" !

She walks around barefoot a lot ;
      they sting her on her stepper
So then her dialogue is salted
      with a little pepper.
And she's old-fashioned so she wants her paybacks,
      eye-for-eye,
Which means that black-and-yellow ____ ____ ____
      is gonna die !

The Yellow Jacket has the pep some others seem to lack.
It's well-disposed to combat and it loves the sneak attack.
She tried the spray-bomb that is guaranteed to kill 'em dead.
A swatter's nearly useless, even when you bash their head.
A hammer, rock or boot heel is too hard on window glass.
The SCISSORS is the only tool that stops 'em in one pass !

First thing, she must discourage buzzing
      'round and 'round the room
With spatula or magazine,
      guitar, dishcloth or broom,
And once they hit the window,
      they are at a disadvantage
And she inflicts some wounds not even
      EMT's could bandage !

With scissors clutched in claw-like hand,
      she closes for the kill,
But even dying, cut in two,
       the buggers won't lie still !
To stop their final wiggle,
      she will snip them all-to-bits .
This gross, inhuman practice
      gives observers shakin' fits .
And then, to keep them nervous,
      grossed-out, shakin' like a feather,
She gathers up the pieces
      and she puts them back together !

She's straight from Stephen King, I think …
      this sis-in-law of mine…
But, barring eight or ten more quirks,
      she's otherwise just fine.
We've tried to understand the ways
      of daddy's youngest daughter,
But Westside people are unique;
      (there's Something in the water !)

OH, WHAT A ... MORNIN'

There's a bright golden haze on the meadow,
Visibility's limited also.
The cornflakes are high in my bowl so that I
Can pour milk that will splash on the table nearby.

       Oh, what a beautiful mornin'.
       Hope it's a beautiful day.
       I've got an uneasy feelin'
       Ev'rythin's goin' astray.

Both the children are standin' like statues.
Try to force them to hustle ... it's no use.
They won't eat their breakfast; their shoes just won't tie.
There's a mess on the rug; tomcat's winkin' his eye.

       Oh, what a beautiful mornin'...
       Start of a treacherous day.
       I've got a dark, broodin' feelin'
       Nothin' is goin' my way.

All the sounds of the house are like Bedlam.
All my thoughts are so frantic, can't catch 'em.
The oatmeal boiled over; the kids wondered why,
And I think that my shirt just got stuck in my fly.

       Oh, what a beautiful mornin'!
       Someday I'll just run away.
       Meanwhile I can't keep from wonderin'
       What next is comin' my way?

       Will it be easy some day?

A friend of ours had a mouse in her house
  And she killed it
    So I titled my poem:

MOUSE IN HER HOUSE

The mouse is dead !
The mouse is dead !
The blinkin', stinkin' mouse is dead !
She bashed it three times on the head.
(I won't repeat the words she said.)
She killed it by herself, it's true.
(It was a "thing" she had to do.)

Frustration reaches fever pitch
And something has to give.
Although it did not cure the glitch,
The mouse has ceased to live.

Some pieces here; some parts were there.
It somehow scattered everywhere.
For one brief moment, all was well;
The outburst left her feeling swell.

A rash and foolish thing to do …
The whole computer's dead now, too.

ODE TO A GENTEEL LADY

Out across the windy prairie where the tumblethistles grow
There's a very special lady you would all be proud to know.
She'll be welcome at your dinner but she'll never stay too long;
With a little warm persuasion, she will join you in a song.
She'll arise at four A.M. to get a little baking done;
Then she'll give it all away to see her neighbors having fun.
She will help wherever needed from the goodness of her heart,
But, to ask about her PET SHOT TRIP would really be unsmart !
At the start it looked so organized, with carriers and all.
It was only forty miles round-trip. The car was sort of small.
For her friend, she went along to keep things going smooth and well.
Soon she'd rue, and long remember, this Trip-to-the-Vet's from Hell.
Put one kitty here, and two in there … the doggies in the back .
(Never mind that these two dogs were midget buffalo, in fact.)
When at last they had it loaded and were rolling down the road,
It was very soon, and then they knew, they had an OVERLOAD !
Cats were yowling for release and not politely taking turns.
Dogs were peering in and getting bloody snoots for their concerns.
With the jostling and the screeching and the scratching
            and the drool …
(Even educated ladies sometimes slip and play the fool.)
But the spatial limitation was what got this lady's goat ;
Putting two big dogs in one car somehow makes them seem to bloat.
Any motion is accompanied with flying haze of hair.
Early-on, our gal remembered why, for pets she does not care.
Doggies shove and crowd and try to see what's passing, left and right.
Half an hour of that can make you feel you've been in quite a fight.
They're incautious where they place their feet; they slobber,
            pant and lick.
Take a hot car, add a dogfart, try to keep from being sick.
Turn your head and hide your eyes when doggy wets Doc's
            dogfood shelf;
Nod agreement with the cussing when he can't control himself.
In a year or so the trip was done; she staggered from the car
With a fleeting thought : one time, perhaps, her "friend"
            will go too far.
For her valor, up and over any normal expectation,
We present this verse of praise and love and thankful
            commendation.

23

"O, O, O ! ... OW, OW, OW !"

My wife is always lady-like; genteel at work or play.
Some women seem to have a knack; they're naturally that way.
She isn't an affected, haughty, prissy kind of wife.
Whatever comes, she takes in-stride and goes on with her life.
So when, one day, she wanted to walk down the basement stair,
Though present, we men didn't feel we needed to be there.
Those seven steps she's done before with no adverse effect.
Why would we think she'd pick this trip to try to break her neck ?
What follows now is hearsay ; no one witnessed the event.
It went so fast, she missed the cause, which was not her intent.
A sliding, thumping, bumping, vocalized by, "O, O, O !"
A Splat ! and then a slow, more painful comment, "Ow, Ow, Ow !"
We rushed to find she'd slipped and must have done a pirouette.
Flat on her back on the concrete floor ... but was she living yet ?
Oh, good ! no worse for wear and tear. Relief showed in our smile.
"Here, take my hand ?" "Oh, no. I think I'll just sit here awhile."
She spurned our efforts to assist. She claims we guffawed loud.
But, bruised and sore, she got herself back up ... genteel,
                and proud.

PUTTING BABY TO SLEEP

The baby gives us signals when she's ready for her nap.
She fusses and she stretches and she throws herself right back.
Then missus grabs a blanket and she rolls the baby tight ...
Makes sure the arms are tucked in so there isn't any slack.
And then, although its possible to bring on sleep by rocking,
(Of course, a little singing helps to occupy her ears,)
It's usually much better if we do a little walking
And even then, we get some squawks and,
                    now and then, some tears.
But often, she just sings along with "Abble dabble doo"
While being packed around the house for six or seven rounds,
And missus does her best : Merle, Waylon, "Tippy-Toein'" too ...
(She's short on lullabys but baby loves those country sounds.)
Well, recently she hit upon a quicker sleep technique.
Instead of C. and W. she tried "Old Rugged Cross".
As everybody knows, "The spirit's willing; flesh is weak."
The contrast soothed the urchin good ... or put her at a loss.
In only one trip round the house, or just a few steps more,
That baby closed her eyes and drifted off to slumberland,
And, while she's not yet old enough to just saw logs and snore,
The speed of her response to sacred music is just grand !
The wife was "on a roll" and tried the same old hymn again.
One brief walk "put her under"; we'll suspend our naptime search.
But as we try to raise her right, before we say "Amen",
We'll have to watch that kid ; I bet she'll fall asleep in church .

REVERIE 1

It was noonday Tuesday, one day past that week of rain in May.
Crop prospects were looking up; we all had pleasant things to say.
Warming sun and gentle breeze and few mosquitos buzzing 'round
Such a moment one can sigh and pause
        and rest from cares unbound.
On the bench beside the Post Office, two retirees sat down
Like a Norman Rockwell picture or a flashback Old Home Town.
As if magnets, they attracted two more senior guys to talk
And a bunch of people passing-by took time to smile and gawk.
Laughing, talking loud and gesturing in camaraderie ...
Just a moment in a million but it meant a lot to me.
I guess nothing quite so quickly warms the cockles of our hearts
As the animated memories of two or more old ... fellows.

REVERIE 2

Within two days of writing up the geezers of our town
I had occasion to observe the women gather 'round.
They congregated, like the men, close to the same old spot,
(You ain't heard nothin' till they get THEIR "conversators" hot !)
The rising, falling, laughing, cooing, blending, clashing talk ...
Like when your barnyard flock has been attacked by chickenhawk !
When I was small, my quiet aunt referred to "hens" and "clucks",
But not the feathered fryers in the yard with geese and ducks.
I've heard the chickenhouse when Leghorn layers get upset,
But which kind makes the loudest squawks, I hesitate to bet.
The energy those women used would tire a man to death.
The gals I talked to afterward weren't even out of breath !

Our friend has too many pets…and too many pet problems.

SEAM RIPPER

You would think you could finish your breakfast in peace
  And be done before things fall apart.
But I guess on a hot Thursday, Seven A.M., August two
  Is a good time to start.
Just two days since I'd taken my mini-rat-terrier
  Off to the vet to be spayed,
As we sat on the sofa, just me and my pup,
  What I saw made me plenty dismayed,
For her sutures had broke, the incision was open,
  Her insides were all falling out !
Sure, I have quilted some and I've altered some clothes
  So I do know what stitching's about.
Still, this job was beyond any sewing I've done ;
  I had best let the vet try again.
What to do ? I SaranWrapped those reeking insides
  As she started to wriggle in pain
And I phoned for the lady who always is there
  With her help and her stiff upper lip.
Could she drive? Could she hurry? And please not complain
  For we still had a fifty-mile trip.
I had called her before, and the neighbor had, too,
  For assistance in hauling our pets.
Her aversion to noise, stink and fuss makes pet-hauling
  As nigh unto Hell as it gets.

Bloody guts on the right; squirming dog on the left …
  Couldn't tear off a strip … no third hand !
So I used the whole roll … didn't work very well …
  Guess next time I'll try "Press-n-Seal" brand.
The SaranWrap was slipping … the dog started biting …
  My driver was crying some, too,
But she never once puked, so I guess
  Kleenex stuffed up her nose was the right thing to do.

She is not known for speeding, but that day she did,
        And I told her, "Go through that red light !"
But I knew, when she stopped, I was pushing my luck.
        This was no time to quibble or fight.

So we got to the vets and we showed her what happened.
        She said, "I dunno why it did,
But we'll stuff her together and stitch her back shut …
        She should make it … she's still just a kid "
The assistant came out, said a bunch of nice things
        And her words gave our heartstrings a tug.
Said how lucky I was to have such a good friend …
        Then she gave my pet driver a hug !

Till the dog moves her bowels, we won't know if she'll live:
        It's a wait that I barely can stand.
And I stopped at the clinic for antibiotic.
        Little S.O.B chewed up my hand !
She's a six hundred dollar pooch … only five pounds .
        All that time and miles, plus the vet bill,
And I bet, when we're done, we'll have "double-or-nothing".
        Pet ownership is SUCH a thrill !

RUDE AWAKENING

At dawn, my covers all were "tooken"
      Which left me feeling quite forsooken.
I bravely rose and made a dash
      To find the firebox full of ash.
Heat surplus of the night before
      Can reach to breakfast, nevermore.
Of course I think it plenty rude
      To yank the quilt and leave me nude
But I won't fuss. I'll let her sleep
      Beneath that cozy blanket-heap
And for my parka I'll be lookin'
      Until the woodstove gets to cookin'.

Zurich, Montana, is known for its quality school … home of the
Bulldogs. The Zurich Association of Parents … ZAP … does an
annual program to honor their teachers.

2001 TEACHER APPRECIATION WEEK – ZURICH

"The time has come," the chairman said, "to talk of many features.
Next week we need to show that we appreciate our teachers."
The fertile minds of ZAP bore down;
      they knew about brainstorming,
And, one by one, a daily run of "Thank You's" started forming.
"We need to find a special treat…a stress-relieving session."
"I have it !" said one gal, and gave her concept full expression.
"Some lady had a booth set up at Fergus County Fair.
She'd rub your neck and shoulders
      while you used her special chair.
Her fee was low, but OH ! how good she made the people feel !"
(With half a dozen teachers, ZAP could get a special deal !)
"A good idea !" "A great idea !" "We'll borrow it from her !"
"We'll do it right at Zurich School ! We'll hire a real masseur !"
No sooner said than done !
      They phoned to get a school appointment
But, as with many good ideas, a fly was in the ointment.
He would not leave his parlor, they discovered with their call.
He charged, for one, as much as ZAP had planned to pay for all !
He would not come to Zurich School, or even to their houses.
He would not rub their necks at all till they removed their blouses !

ZAP gave up neck-and-shoulder rubs.
      For new ideas they're probing.
But, how they smile to think about the teachers all disrobing !

The Zurich Association of Parents ... ZAP ... asked me to help
them build cute wooden pencilholders for all their teachers. Shaped
like an apple with wormholes on top to hold pencils, each had two
leaves that I was to fashion. Only later, I learned that our
lumberyard sold pre-shaped "leaves" at four cents each.

2002 TEACHER APPRECIATION WEEK -- ZURICH

I think that I shall never see
More trouble than an apple tree;
A tree that sits on teacher's desk
To keep her pencils safe at rest.
A tree whose leaves don't quake so good
Because, of course, they're made of wood.
A tree whose leaves were sanded down
To make their edges smooth and round.
The sander, an electric belt
Which, touched by fingers, could be felt
As fingernails were ground away
To make two dozen leaves a day.
Now, gummed-up sander, worn-out belt
In wallet pocket will be felt.
The leaves, "glue biscuits" proved to be,
From lumberyard ... four bucks per "c".
This poem was made by foolish me
But, next time, God can make the tree.

SOAPBAR BLUES

I bought a bar of Ivory to wash my face and hands.
I know it's good for carving, too, but I had no such plans.
  I put it in the soapbar dish for anyone to lather.
I also got a bar of Dial in case someone would rather.

  Within a day, my girl inquired why I had duplicated.
I said, when soap in shower was gone, a ready fresh bar waited.
  We went along about a week, my boy, my girl and me.
But someone took a different bar. That meant we'd opened three.
  I won't complain, but I have found one dish/three bars unhandy.
And yet, a choice, three kinds of soap, most folks consider dandy.
  But something happened just tonight it grieves my heart to tell.
My Ivory fell on the floor and fractured all-to-pieces.
  I've seen soap melt or crumble, soak away or slip or slide,
But Ivory that splinters ? Was this soap bar petrified ?

  I do not know who dropped it there, the shards and slivers scattered.
I want the guilty one to know: there's ONE who thinks it mattered!

*   *   *   *

SOAPBAR BLUES REVISITED

When I was home some time ago,
        I found the soapdish loaded.
The Ivory fell on the floor
        And ... big surprise ... exploded !
Now I have learned my lesson well :
        Don't let the soapbar fall.
But, in the soapdish this trip home
        There ain't no soap at all !

                    Marisa Mailand

A man grows accustomed to having "the woman" around, taking care of certain jobs. Her absence, even brief, leads to new appreciation.

TEST OF DEVOTION

You left me on Thursday, right around noon;
      I hated to see you go,
But I had to be back on the job until six
      So I didn't yet miss you so.

The beans in the crockpot were ready by supper;
      I had me quite a feast.
Then my buddy came over to watch some TV
      Was I lonesome ? Not in the least.

When he left, I suspended doing my chores ...
      Found a pirated v.c.r.
With three movies on-board, which I watched until two ...
      Not my best plan-of-action, by far.

Then at six, I got up for a long day at work,
      And a busy day I had.
On my mini-lunch break, FedEx brought our fresh fish
      Which we re-froze before it went bad.

Did I mention ? that morning we had a hard rain
      So I reckon a few things got wet
But I didn't take time to examine for damage.
      If there was, it'll be that way yet.
Friday supper, I finished the homemade bread
      And all the soft butter was gone
So for Saturday lunch, all the spread was rock-hard,
      Plus, I had to weed-whip the back "lawn".
But I first did a couple postponed little jobs,
      With delays by the telephone bell.
Then I lunched on "store" burger buns, crackers and cheese
      And the last of the baked beans as well.

Now I'm eyeing those family-size cans of Chow Mein
      That you want me to eat on-my-own,
And I might dine on spinach and meatball stew
      Till my regular cook returns home.

And I'm eyeing the clock; those black hands barely creep
    …there's still twenty-four hours to go.
But on weekends, our one café closes up shop .
    I might miss you more than I know.

Yes, I finished the leftovers, just as you said,
    And I offered the scraps to the cat
And I piled all your dishes up, safe in the sink.
    Could a man love his mate more than that ?

   *   *   *   *

THANKS, MOM

I do not want my milk jugs rinsed, nor soup containers washed.
I do not want wax paper saved, nor breakfast boxes squashed.
I do not want my peelings dried ; I want to pitch them wet.
I like the casual approach ; no neater will I get.
I like some lint upon my floor … I put it there myself.
Don't dust the corners anymore or (Horrors !) closet shelf !
Don't clean SaranWrap or, I swear, I'll eat it … every bite !
I won't cook rice for breakfast . Crunchy LIFE is priced just right !
I thank the Lord that I'm your son ; I love you like no other.
I vow to make it through this life, my fond, protective Mother.

   *   *   *   *

Sitting on my front stoop one evening, I was watching
the tulips and day lilies and creeping jenny fold their
petals at the end of the day. Remarkable !

WRAP UP

    I never want to go to bed
    Before the flowers do.
    It bothers me to call it quits
    Before the day is through.
    And though I know I'll wake
    Before tomorrow's blooms, no doubt,
    I like to watch them "close up shop"
    Before the lights go out.

CHAPTER TWO

HOME ON THE RANGE

*　　*　　*　　*　　*

Poet Fred Liese said it best :

"Harlem ... is the most 'Western' town in Montana. If there was a more western town, I'd move to it !"

COTTONWOOD BLUES

There's a cottonwood tree in my neighbor's backyard
     And it hangs halfway over my fence.
While I'm ready for my share of deadfall and leaves,
     The percentages just don't make sense.
Those prevailing west winds drive the leaves all my way …
     I buy extra trash bags and I rake …
But the branches that seem to drop off all the time …
     (Can a cottonwood make a mistake ?)
For it seems, hardly ever, they fall on his side
     But forever, they're falling on mine.
I suspect gravity has a spare helping hand
     With behavior that "crosses the line".
In the balance of next-door relations, I think
     Finger-pointing and snitching are vile,
But consider their size and their weight ; are you sure
     Branches always would fall in one pile ?

Starting about 2004, Harlem has been deluged, from time to time, with used-car ads, one-page boxholders, hand-written, urging people with credit problems to call for "guaranteed financing".

BLINDSIDED

The guy who came up with the hand-written ad
    That we get in our mailbox each week,
        Though his grammar and script are incredibly bad,
        Does a service I think is unique.
He purports to sell cars to the broke, down, and out;
    He can get them financed, come what may,
        And the thrill of the new car he's talking about
        Is one quick toll-free phonecall away.
I assume he's successful at peddling his wares ;
    There's a half-dozen copycats now
        And while many folks cuss, rant and rip out their hairs,
        I am glad that he showed them all how.
For each salesman just scribbles one side of the page
    Leaving hundreds of multi-hued blanks
        Which most people throw out in disgust and outrage …
        It's scratchpaper for which I give thanks !
For the job of the poet is writing down verse
    Which he'll change many times till it flows,
        Using pencil or pen till it's striking and terse …
        (Rhymes can take lots more paper than prose.)
So to all scribbling salesmen who flood us with ads :
    Keep 'em coming, but one-sided, please.
        I just love the free scratchpaper three times a week …
        (I just hope we don't run out of trees !)

Hi there, BIG Sale oac
Call now!
Over 800 New and Used.
Drive your dream Car today oac
No Down, oac 90 Days oac
Divorce, BK, Repo, 1st time?
No Problem! oac 😊 Call Now
Financing gaurenteed! oac
Turn down? Trade Not Paid?
No problem! oac
All Aplications Acepted. oac
Sale Ends Soon, Call Sparky
tollfree oac 1 800 XXX XXXX
Besure and ask for Sparky
😊

When a young friend needed "an historic event" for a class
project, we put together this account , to which she was an eyewitness.

ELEVATOR FIRE

When the elevator closed, we had a fine historic site
But we had no funds to keep it or repair it tourist-right,
So it sat and rotted and became a place for kids and drunks
And a lot of cats and pigeons and some spiders, mice and skunks.
By and by, somebody lit a campfire on the wooden floor.
It appeared we wouldn't have out tall museum anymore.
Cops and kids and firefighters and a lot of people watched.
On this job of civic betterment, they didn't want it botched.
So they stood and watched and talked until the power pole got lit
But they couldn't squirt it down for fear they'd get electric-bit.
Then the autos in the carlot started getting blistered paint.
When the service station fuel tank lit, I felt a little faint.
If it blew, the burning fuel could torch our whole main business street
And the clean-up of our hometown would be pretty much complete.
So our firefighters did their job and saved our little town.
By next morning, our historic elevator tumbled down.
When the lights came on, one city block was looking pretty bleak
And the elevator smoldered for about another week.
Then, for days, the homeless pigeons flew and circled in the air
And the homeless spiders, cats and drunks
were scattered here and there.

Rani Kolar

KEVIN CROSSING

If you spend some time in Kevin, (and I don't know why you would.)
Finish up your business and go home, the way you know you should.
But if circumstances force you to be there some extra time,
Ask someone to tell about the famous "tow truck" railroad line.

Now, a crossing is no place to dawdle or procrastinate.
It's an easy way to join a bunch of folks who met their fate.
But it happened that two boys who drove their car across the track
Got hung up right in the middle : no more forward ... no more back.

It's a sticky spot to be in, but a tractor or a truck
And a little tug or boost can put you right back on your luck.
But this time, the train was coming ; rescue time was going fast
Though the boys had wished it otherwise, they walked away at last.

In a moment, train and car would meet ; the train was sure to win.
But in Kevin, life was slower then . The boys began to grin,
For the engine slowed and stopped before the terrible collision
And the engineer climbed down to offer choice in this decision.

"Do you boys need help?" he calmly asked. The boys said,
        "Yes, we do !"
"Hook this towrope to your car and somewhere on the engine, too."
With a roar the giant diesel gently pulled the auto free
And the boys were glad to thank the best train man they'd ever see.

Using common sense, big trouble was avoided on that day.
 One man paused to help, and both the car and engine pulled away.
There are many tales in Kevin if you take the time to check.
Some less pleasant than the time the car and railroad didn't wreck.

JOPLIN CROSSING

Matthew, Zane and the other hired guy
Hitched the lowboy to the semi and they really made 'er fly.
It's a '68 Freightliner, busted window, two-tone green,
And it's big and rough and ugly : it's a cowboy's dream machine.
They have used this rig enough that they began to name it "Dandy"
And they called it several other names ...
        just now they don't seem handy.
If you ride the clutch a little hard, you get an awful stench
And you gotta shift to lowrange with a knucklebuster wrench.

Zane was eight years old, and "helping out",
        and looking for some fun.
(When you only haul a tractor, you expect an easy run.)
they were doing really well ; Zane wasn't even bossing
when the trailer got high-centered at the railroad crossing.

Now, the trailer blocked the roadway and the truck was on the track
And they couldn't pull it forward and they couldn't haul it back
So they turned it here and there and they did a little jerking
But no matter what they tried to do, their plan wasn't working.
As the train was coming down the track the fellers started sweating.
"Let's decide what to do and then let's get to getting !"
Should they run, or give it one more try ? They studied one another.
The boss would be upset, and the wives ? Oh, Brother !
With the truck, the borrowed trailer, and the tractor up on board
It was just a little more than these three cowboys could afford.
Plus, a loaded trailer's neither quick nor easy to unhitch,
And who wants to pay for someone's rig
        that's scattered down the ditch ?

Dandy's clutch was slipping, smoking ;
        piston sleeve was clanking too.
They continued jamming gears, no prayers or cussing left to do.
Inch by inch, they worked it off the track.
        When Amtrak thundered through
Passengers and our three cowboys got a very closeup view.
And to make it double-bad, as soon as Amtrak whistled past
Came a mile of B-N freight train that was rolling just as fast.

Zane considered just how close they came;
        his blood had turned to ice.
"Just as well we got 'er busted loose, or they'd have hit us twice !"
Well, they tied up traffic for an hour, and when they had it done,
One and all were pretty well convinced : There ain't no easy run !

THE HARRISONS HAVE IT

The cautious folks of Harrison are 'way ahead of US ;
They got Homeland Security without the cost or fuss.
It took cooperation and a bold, creative view
When they agreed to plan as one ... all hundred sixty-two !
Three highways go to Harrison ... the railroad tracks as well .
No harbor yet, or airfield strip, as far as we can tell.

A few miles north of Harrison on route 359
You have to cross the railroad tracks ...
      you'll see the crossing sign.
And if you look south down the tracks about a hundred feet,
You'll see a curiosity that might be hard to beat.
Built right across the track, a big steel gate, (I think it's green),
Chained up and locked, but there's no guard
      or gateman to be seen,
But on one side, a mailbox stands ...
      who knows the reason why
Unless it holds the gate key for the train to slip on by.
In days of old, the fireman could have stayed to close the gate,
Then caught a ride on the caboose to save a lengthy wait.
But now, there's no more fireman; they don't use
      the red caboose,
And gates left hanging open are of very little use.

Because we don't know how it works, we have to speculate
On how the folks of Harrison best-utilize their gate.
If engineers, themselves, unlock to roll on down the track,
Then, chaining up, they waste some time,
      hiking forth and back.
Should Harrison suspect a plot or breached security,
They'd simply leave their steel gate locked
      and hide away the key.
If engineers must write in for permission to pass through,
They'd park, and wait, across the road and
      block that traffic, too.
When mail arrives by truck or train,
      there's bound to be delay
While those in charge decide who gets to use the right-of-way.

And if they use a cellphone to ensure the track is clear,
I hope reception works a little better there, than here.
Most likely, there's another locked gate somewhere
          down the line.
You don't "highball" through Harrison; you learn to take your time.

I wrote the mayor of Harrison ; so far, there's no reply.
If that mail comes by road or rail, I know the reason why.
If you should visit Harrison, prepare yourself to wait,
And after leaving Harrison, remember : close the gate.

ON THE MEND

When I was young, my teacher said, "Use language that is vivid !"
I practiced hard, because my normal way would make her livid.
    At first, the search for adjectives and adverbs seemed too tough
But then, recycled cusswords proved : there'll always be enough.
    So, having mastered forceful speech, I turned to adding color.
My florid phrases far surpassed the pale, the vague, the duller.
    I next tried convoluted eloquence and had a ball !
I got so good, no one I knew could understand at all !
    But then one day...that fateful day...the day all scribes abhor,
I used my last superlative, and hadn't any more !
    The tank was dry; the purse was flat; the pocket, limp and empty.
With nothing past "Good–Better–Best", no more plateaus to tempt me
    My writing slumped, my mood went black, my thoughts wild and fantastic.
I thought I'd see a "shrink" before committing something drastic.
    I said, "Hey Doc ! How do you work ? How often do you charge,
And can you fix me up before your statement gets too large ?"
    "You talk, I listen," he replied. "A cure may take us years.
We need to probe the reasons for your problems, hopes and fears.
    The charge? Ah yes. What is it worth to function more like normal?
I'll work with your H.M.O. for a plan that's fair and formal."
    "Well Doc, I'll see you 'round," I said. I'm glad you filled me in.
I don't have 'shrink insurance' and my bankroll's gettin' thin.
    The poems I write are full of all my problems, hopes and fears.
It's what I've used to entertain the people all these years
    My audience has always furnished first-rate therapy
I talk, they listen, laugh and clap ...and they work quick ...and free!
    So I'll just mosey back to work. You've sure been awful nice
I think I learned my lesson so I won't be askin' twice."
    We read about new breakthroughs, but the price is always high.
For most of us, I guess we learn to live with it ... or die.
    We'll always be a little short of Magic Bullet cures,
But ain't it fun to see someone with problems worse than yours ?

PAPERBOY

I never received my newspaper this week.
      The "kid" from the "home" brings it by.
I try to be there to say "Thank You" each time
      When he rears back his arm and lets fly.
The paper's a free weekly shopper's report ;
      Every Wednesday the ads are all new.
Well, I think he gets paid for his time and his work
      And it gives the kid something to do.
He's my regular "paperboy" week after week ;
      Someone else walks the route overstreet.
And I guess what impresses me most ?   Now and then
      He appears to be "totally beat".
There's a droop to his face and he shambles along,
      Shoulders slumping and arms to his feet.
Like an Atlas, the paperbag crushes him down;
      Only death could make his day complete.
As he goes, he sheds papers as quick as he can,
      Too exhausted to fling at my door.
He's been known to deliver to fencepost and bush ;
      (He goes home when his bag holds no more.)
So, to lighten his load and to cheer his bad days,
      (I would bet he's ignored by most folks,)
I say "Thank You", real big, when I see him drag past,
      (Though he's more used to teasing and jokes.)
And the change, (only brief), to his forty-odd years
      Shines out from his huge, gap-toothed grin,
And I think it recharges us both just a bit.
      Then he shuffles off downstreet again.
So I guess, for the paper I'm lacking this week,
      I'll hike down to the store afterwhile.
I believe what I miss is not news or the ads,
      But that all-over, tail-wagging smile.

ROYAL CHICKEN

It was time once again for the plans to begin
      For the neighborhood Sunday night feed.
Two young hens lost their life, and our chef told his wife,
      "With the sweetcorn, that's all we will need."
From a week baling hay, he was set for a day
      Of relaxing with friends and a beer.
It was his day to cook and his first chance to hook up
      The brand-new rotisserie gear.
He's a "barbecue king" ; he can do anything
      From a bird to a fish to a steak,
And it's his biggest treat to watch hungry folks eat
      (And leave compliments right at the plate.)
So he skewered the meat and he turned up the heat ;
      Then he went to do last-minute chores,
But all senses awoke when he saw clouds of smoke
      From the grill, as he closed the barn doors.
Ten short minutes it took for those chickens to cook
      At a scorching 700 degrees !
Sure, the breaker box blew ... major grill meltdown, too,
      And fowl "clinkers" as black as you please !
When the birds lost their glow, we all knew they would go
      To the trash barrel, quick as a wink.
And the phrases we heard ! Not a single new word,
      But unique combinations, I think.
It was shameful to tell, they booked passage to Hell
      On that maiden rotisserie ride,
And our chef hung his head ... thawed lasagna instead
      And nursed serious hurt to his pride.
Years of dinners prepared, well-presented and shared,
      Never mentioned in verse or in song,
But, commit one small gaffe, they point, snicker and laugh
      And they headline "The Meal That Went Wrong" !

I'm a retired High School teacher. As I drive up and down
U.S. Highway 2, I am reminded of many of my former
students. Since 1952, the V.F.W. has erected nearly 3000
white crosses along Montana's highways. In our area, you
can count almost one cross for every mile.

STOPPING BY CROSSES
ON A LONELY ROAD

Whose cross is this, I think I know.
He was my student long ago.
He brought to class his wit and cheer,
His pranks and laughing, bright hello.

I must look foolish standing here,
My need and purpose both unclear.
Some drivers do a double-take
To see me wipe away a tear.

I missed his funeral and wake,
Felt sorrow for his parents' sake
And for his friend, who fell asleep
And for the life he'll never make.

I know these crosses, and I weep …
So many in my memory keep.
The slaughtered lambs forever sleep.
The pain of loss of friends runs deep.

This is actually Loxi's poem but she never finished it.
I helped her as much as I could.

TIME CAPSULE

In seventy-six we bought a house ... the first we ever got.
We knew it had some problems. ...Well, okay, the shack was shot !
Storm windows gone, no paint, no screens, the whole darn roof was leaky,
The furnace was a "ten-percenter", back stairs loose and creaky,
Some doors were gone, some broken, small gas stoves in every corner,
Bad wiring, too-few outlets ... this place couldn't be forlorner !
One thing the owner said : "The downstairs bathroom stool is 'iffy'.
Light duty's fine ; big jobs can overflow in just a jiffy!"
But it was down the list of jobs that needed our attention ;
It sort-of worked. I hate to plumb. The pot was in suspension.

We owned our mansion free and clear and started restoration :
New roof, new paint, new carpet, wall and ceiling insulation.
We added on a couple rooms, a girl and boy as well .
A working home, and comfy, but you'd hardly call it "swell".
The house, pre-'40, once a rural schoolhouse moved on-site.
They added-on at least five times and never got it right.
A rental, once five power meters graced the basement hall.
(Old tales from former tenants tend to cause your skin to crawl.)

For twenty-seven years that cranky toilet gave us grief.
Each time it flushed without a flood we sighed with sweet relief.
But, by and by, we had to face replacement or repair.
I bravely set my mind to reconstruct our antique chair.

51

(I'd like to say the first payload went smoothly swooshing thru it,
But after more than fifty years, the old throne couldn't do it.
We know "H.W." marked it good in 2-8-52.
Since then, I wonder at the times this thundermug passed through.
It tried to flush okay, and didn't flood … for that I'm grateful.
I wonder if the old potmaker cast-in something hateful ?)

At last, the twenty-ninth of May, the year, two-thousand three,
I overhauled our toilet … top of list … EMERGENCY,
And 'way down deep inside I found a bottlecap had jammed
And ever since, at least one-half the normal flow was dammed.
I had to show it to my pal, my patient, loving wife
Who pitched right in and shared the past three decades of her life.
Did that obstruction represent a capsule of the past ?
She looked it over, smiled a bit, and calmly spoke at last.
I think she waxed as wistful as she's yet been known to get :
"That bottlecap has put up with an awful lot of   !"

(That's the part she never finished.)

I like potato chips. I once got a bag in a new flavor and discovered that it was awful. I believe when one is dissatisfied with a product, one should let the manufacturer know.

VIVA SABOR !
Ripples Chile Limon flavor Potato Chips

Yes, we all prefer some changes
      and variety in snacks
And I guess that's why they sell them
      in a rainbow choice of sacks,
But when Ripples put the Chile Limon chip
      on grocers' shelves,
Pardon me ... the need is great
      for Ripples to excuse themselves !
By itself the chili pepper
      is a lovely spice, I think,
And, with lemon or alone,
      the lime can make a dandy drink.
But the combination ... chili-lime ...
      while radical and new,
Conjures up the recollection
      of a nasty bout of flu
Or a late carouse of strong libations
      hurriedly brought back ...
Retrospect of bad experience
      of which there is no lack.
Now, in matters of chip business,
      it's not my place to rebuke,
But why would someone buy a chip
      that tastes so much like puke?

I sent a copy of my poem to Ripples, and they <u>never</u> <u>wrote</u> <u>back</u> !

WOODSPLITTER BLUES

My neighbor splits his firewood and stores it dry and handy.
He bought a big hydraulic rig from some guy in Big Sandy.
To try it out required a load of blocks which he acquired
And eagerly began to split … he was a man inspired !
He picked a chunk of cottonwood … a heavy, knotty section.
He had no steel-toed boots to give protection and deflection.
The law of gravity prevailed ; the chunk of wood, it dropped,
And did not pause nor tarry till upon his toe it stopped.

My neighbor knew he had been struck a fracture-causing blow.
As soon as meet, he hastened in, that his goodwife should know.
"Goodwife," said he. "My toe, you see, should have an X-ray picture,
And when it starts to ache and throb, some circulation stricture ?"

"Indeed," goodwife replied, "I do prescribe a trip to Havre,
But do not keen and whimper so. You're not yet a cadaver !"
Enlisting aid from clergy and a fast blue Plymouth with her,
My neighbor rode to hospital all in a painful dither.

"Three places broke ! Three places broke !"
                    the doctor, he did cackle.
He wrapped it up, and all the while, the fragments, they did crackle.
Now teacher lectures from his chair, his toe upraised for comfort.
No hiking, skating, skiing now, or any other dumb sport.

Boots ordered, now this teacher knows each lesson is a gain :
Mass + Velocity + Pedal Digit = PAIN !
The students hope their Prof has learned the laws of physics well :
A log, set free to gravity, can hit, and hurt, like the dickens !

THE FOUNTAIN AT TURNER

In Turner, it's the Old Gym where the people congregate
Celebrating big events like Jane and Harlan's "Golden Date"
And I might have missed it but, with luck, I wrangled an invite
To provide some entertainment for the neighbors there that night.
So I took along some verses to promote a jolly mood
And a hearty appetite ! (Those Turner ladies sure know food !)
And I took along my missus, (also called "the better half").
She can keep a crowd a-goin' with her bright, infectious laugh.

Just before the time to start the show, I took a little break
In the "Cowboys" room right near the back door,
                    just for comfort's sake.
When I'd done my thing, I leaned down and depressed the flusher handle
And a waterspout gushed from the bowl like some weird liquid candle !

It behaved how you'd expect a living, breathing thing would do,
Leaping up a foot, and arching over, landing on my shoe !
There I stood, amazed, with "squooshy foot" and "soggy pantleg" too,
With no time to dry off prior to my big on-stage debut.

It's a good thing young Maloney had some trouble with the mike,
Since he kept the crowd's eyes off my damp leg, there's a kid I like !
I suppose somebody wondered at my wet tracks on the floor
But those Turner folks are quite forgiving ; some things they ignore.

Now, that big All Class Reunion budget must have caused some stress ;
Sprucing up the whole town forced them to accomplish more, with less,
And, with water scarce, a big display they'd veto, to a man,
So they built their City Fountain … at the Old Gym … in the "can" ?

Shortly after my "Fountain" poem appeared in the newspaper
I received a phonecall from a somewhat irate reader. She
complimented me on the writing, but questioned my facts.
It was not the Turner ladies, but the Hogeland ladies who had
prepared the feed, and what was I going to do about it ?

SORRY, WRONG COOKIE

Of all the lessons I have learned, the one that really "took"
Was the one that warned of dire results if I ever crossed The Cook.
So as I pussyfoot through life, avoiding such a gaffe,
I try to jolly-up all cooks with poems to make them laugh.
But, even cautious poets commit inadvertent sin
When they "shoot off their poem" before final results are in.
My "Turner Fountain" poem thanked Turner ladies for the food
So I would come across polite, and not thoughtless or rude.
But now I learn it's Hogeland ladies I should have been thanking
To save my fanny from a kick, a chewing or a spanking.
 Of course, I've sampled Turner grub; those ladies cook good, too,
But I believe one must place credit where that credit's due.
At first, to play it safe, I thought I'd call them "Big Flat Ladies".
One glance, and my chief editor, (my Missus,) "gave me Hades" !
 "You can't use such a phrase, or else you better knock on wood.
Although it's technically correct, it sure don't sound so good."
With cap-in-hand, I called on Tricia. "Please print a retraction.
I fear a flurry of unrest : a Punitive Reaction !"
So here's to Hogeland Lutheran ladies : thank you very much !
(I hope this verse is cute enough to get me out of Dutch.)

A second phonecall advised that I was forgiven ... for now.

CHAPTER THREE

THE WILD COUNTRYSIDE

* * * * *

Symbiotic relationship with crops and livestock, confidence born of necessity, live-and-let-live attitude, tough love, sense of humor, understatement, respect and loyalty, appreciation of the beauty of Nature ... all these are part of the western personality. The pioneer spirit lives on!

BEST GUESS

"That's the last of them, Dear … loaded, ready to ship.
          What do you think this year's set will weigh ?"
(We all try to predict how the steers average out
          When they go to the scales the next day.)
Our trucker has seen plenty beef on the hoof ;
          We have lots of respect for that man
When he writes down his vote. But my wife, bless her heart,
          Guesstimates it as well as she can.
"Oh now, Honey, you'll only embarrass yourself
          With a number so far off the mark.
You know they won't average nearly that high ;
          You're just taking a shot in the dark."
But in spite of my training, my offered advice
          And my telling her she's 'way too high,
She will hang tough … no change … let's await the results.
          (It's enough to make grown cowboys cry.)
Since she judged them 'way heavy, I tried to help out …
          Held the light ones to get her on track.
What the heck was she doing ? She caught all my culls
          And she shoved all the light ones right back !
Let 'em go. She must learn. When experience shows
          I'll be satisfied ; I'm not to blame.
She'll become laughing stock … reputation destroyed …
          What a way to bring shame to your name !
Last year … what was her guess ? She was just five pounds off ?
          (We guys missed it by twenty or so.)
And now this year ? By golly ! Just five pounds light, too !
Gee, I'd rather not hear women crow !
I'm downright disappointed. With my expertise
          I get nothing to take credit for.
If she guesses like that, I'll just keep my advice
          And I won't help her out anymore !

For Les & Jackie Eide

BRANDIN' OVER EASY by Matt Eide

The outfit I work for is split up some and scattered all over the place
But Marias River country is what we all consider home base.
The bossman left us staffed to the hilt with the best help he could get
In my opinion, just high-grade hooligans workin' this cow outfit.
Brandin' time was upon us once the calvin' season was through.
I had the job of gatherin' up the North Side brandin' crew.
With a hundred miles to drive before the sun hit our sleepy eyes,
With every yawn we greeted the dawn. What a lucky bunch of guys!
Three fellers and a Redhead Gal ... four thermoses and a purse ...
All crammed into what could easy be a cowboy brandin' hearse !
Wes ran the gearshift now and then. I kept 'er rollin' kinda straight.
I'm sure the horses in the trailer out back admired our steady gait.
We made 'er to the ranch with Redhead's dignity no worse for wear,
(Mostly 'cause she has the disposition of a wounded grizzly bear.)
We hit the ground a-runnin', finished brandin' without a hiccup,
Then we squeeze back in the motorized 5th hitch
              we sometimes call a pickup.
Our sunvisor cowgirl air freshener bit off more than she could chew
When she tried to tame the ripe bouquet
            of our tight-knit brandin' crew !
About Fort Benton, they voted for beer by unanimous consensus ;
Bein' weak in that department, I just abandoned my defenses.
Just a few miles out from Chester, my doggone cellphone rings ;
It's my little darlin, askin', would I bring eggs and "a few little things"?
I hemmed and hawed and looked around and muttered,
            "I guess we could."
(A grocery stop with this bunch sure wasn't thinkin' real good !)
We hit the Thriftway lot; I said, "I'll be just a little while."
But they followed me in, in high spirits, spurs jinglin' down the aisle.
Wes grabs a Slim Jim, smiles, and cracks it...Whap !...
            right on Redhead's butt.
I hollered, "Hey ! Quiet down now and quit behavin' like a nut !"
Wes hooks a pack of Stayfree, spins, and whips 'em at my head.
I slid 'em back on the Corn Flakes shelf as my face was turnin' red.
The checker threw me dirty looks when I hauled my stuff in line.
I wondered if "Grocery Store Abuse" might draw some kind of a fine !

The only place left to haul that grub was the trailer's overhead tack.
TwoDot couldn't reach it ... unless he stuck his head
        through the crack.
While I went lookin' for a tarp and a tiedown strap or two,
Old TwoDot nibbled up a recipe that looked like Omelet Stew.
With a horse that chews up vittles, there wasn't much that I could do,
But I doubt I'll shop for groceries again
        with a beered-up brandin' crew !

A ROMP THROUGH THE CHICKENS

The "thing" about a chicken coop
        is not the noise or "pip" or croup.
It's not egg-gathering every day
        or keeping varmint types at bay.
Some don't mind cluckers underfeet,
        though every fall they look un-neat.
Loose feathers floating everywhere
        and parts that should be covered, bare.
But, while they play with lots of pep,
        you must be careful where you step,
And rolling in your grassy yard
        is very, very, very hard.

Stop and consider, if you would,
        how much the chicken does that's good.
The rooster crows to start the day;
        you dream, somehow this job will pay.
The bugs and hoppers they consume
        saves work with swatter, spray and broom.
For breakfast, eggs ten different ways.
        Ignore that "no cholesterol" craze.)
The peep of chicks so soft and warm
        belies their cannibalistic charm.
The healthful boost of noodle soup
        when illness makes your spirits droop.
Fried chicken dinner ! What a treat !
        And gravy biscuits can't be beat !

Respect your chickens, Heaven's sake
      without eggs how would bakers bake ?
No work for that egg-suckin' dog,
      and what about your Christmas nog ?
For those with philosophic bent,
      the barnyard hen is heaven-sent !
Did egg or chick come first on-scene ?
      Is every rooster mad-dog mean ?
Are clucks forever on-the-peck
      until you wring their scrawny neck?
One plus from their road-crossing bit :
      the POOF of feathers when they're hit !
The search for fun is never hard
      with chickens flocking in your yard.
Their football shape is fun to punt,
      though some folks frown on such a stunt.
It's wild to watch them flip and flop
      because you gave their neck a chop.
The false alarms and constant clucking.
      The singeing and pinfeather plucking.
One more way to abuse and trick 'em :
      Just call the dog and holler "Sic 'em !"

And yet, when all is said and done,
      their claim to fame boils down to one.
For fifty years, I still can tell
      there's fowl nearby, just by the smell.
The "thing" about a chicken coop …
      is poop !

DIETARY LAWN GROOMING

It was only three days after being advised
      How to clear droppings off of my lawn.
Doctor Fred said a bacon grease marinade
      Should guarantee those foul lumps would be gone
And I certainly would not dispute his advice,
      Though I think it a bit premature ;
For the guy on a diet who doesn't eat bacon,
      There's also a "lawn cigar" cure.
With a little more patience and "toughlove" approach,
      I believe I have hit on a plan.
It is simple, humane, economical too,
      And if I did it, anyone can !
In our neighborhood there are some "robber dogs" loose ;
      Every day they check pet feeding trays.
Every pet owner tends to feed more than enough ;
      The excess invites visits from strays.
Lately I, and my neighbors, feed only what's needed ;
      The pet welcome mat was pulled in
So when guests come around to partake of free lunch,
      They discover the pickin's are thin.
Well, I have to admit that I feed table scraps …
      Bits of fat, rind and gristle as well …
And I reckon, although it might pass through quite fast,
      It would still have that rich, meaty smell.
As I said, just this morning I looked out to see
      One of those robber dogs by my truck.
Chowing down on once-digested second-hand pet treats
      And proud of his foraging luck.
So I got double duty from trimmings of meat   ,
      Which is not to belittle Doc Liese.
He suggested recycling ; we re-trained these dogs.
      Pass the do-do, please; hold bacon grease.

DON'T APRIL – FOOL YOUR MAMA

One calf, just two weeks old, got lost about the middle of March.
I put my whole crew on alert to conduct a thorough search.
There ain't been rustlers in these parts for many a peaceful year
So, when a calf just disappears, you don't know what to fear.
We didn't have to search alone ; the cow was searching too.
She felt so bad, I had to figure something I could do.
There's nothing more pathetic than a frantic, calfless cow.
I paired her up with an orphan ... the best I could do for now.
We looked at every coulee, bush and hole around the place.
Each day we thought we'd see a smile on some fat coyote's face.
We looked a week and more. Without some water, milk and feed ...
Well ... nothin' in this cow business was ever guaranteed.

Then one day I was feedin', loadin' hay bales off the stack.
I saw, deep-down, a little space ... light shinin' through a crack
And, wedged in tight, between the rows, that little calf was stuck.
Curiosity had got him in ... then, he ran out of luck.
Dried out and weak ... or dead ? I reached with very little hope.
Ha ! To catch and drag him to his Ma, I had to use my rope !
She snuffled, licked and mumbled some ...
        he'd been a long time gone.
Then she decided they could share ... the orphan and her son.
He jumped straight for Ma's "dinner pail" and then he got right to it.
We dragged him off in a little while for fear he'd overdo it.
I checked the calendar to figure how long he'd been gone.
Eleven days in his "squeeze chute", and the next day ...
        was April One !

One cold, gray, windy November day in 1978, I was working
in the yard, and Slim Ragsdale went by. I thought I ought to
say a few words. It took me three hours and 25 years to write them down.

FALL CHORES

Howdy, Slim.
Fancy rig !
Finally hittin' the trail.
Took ya long enough.
Been a rough ride.
You always was a tough sonofagun.
… you and them mules.
No sense stringin' 'er out.
Bet you was awful tired of it.
Freda, too.
Well, I gotta cut up a pile of kindlin'.
Could be one of them hard winters.
I dunno.
Sky's awful gray an' heavy.
Maybe it's that ol' wind.
Just cuts right thru a fella.
Gotta find my longhandles.
Brrr ! Them poor California folks !
Sure as heck gonna need more wood.
And lookit them geese.
They ain't foolin' around.
They're hightailin' south !
Wish we could all do 'er.
Naah … that'd be too easy !
You drew a pretty good crowd.
Me ? I guess not.
Hafta shave and change clothes.
Too late to shake yer hand anyhow.
I think you picked a good time to bail off.
Good day for a buryin'.
Adios, Slim.

FAREWELL

My sister had a weaner pig ;
  She loved it very well.
She thought it was her buddy
  As near as we could tell.

All spring and summer, by the hour,
  She talked and laughed and played
And bonded with that growing pig.
  (We slowly grew dismayed,)

For in the fall, to feed us all,
  That pig would have to die.
We feared that sis would fall apart
  And protest, wail and cry.

Then Pa, enroute across the yard
  To fetch the knives and gun,
Found sis, conversing with the pig
  Whose life was nearly done.

He walked close by the pen
  To lend a sympathetic ear.
His little girl would lose her friend ;
  He wanted to be near.

But girls are made of sterner stuff
  Than some choose to believe.
The fact is, darn few ranch girls
  Wear their heart upon their sleeve.

His step was light, his hearing keen.
  He heard his darling say,
"Too bad, pig." (Not one tear.)
  "Pa's gonna butcher you today."

THE HOLE PRINCIPLE

People figured it out down in Old New Orleans
        more than 200 years in the past :
When you dig out a hole where there's high water table,
        your hole will fill up pretty fast.
So their graveyards have burial plots, sure enough,
        but their "holes" go up, not down.
They set vaults and crypts right on top of the ground
        to maintain a dry ghost town.

Now, in Circle, Montana, the people don't fear
        that their water table's too high
But that principle ... "holes" can be built down OR up ...
        is still possible to apply.
So when it came time to install the ranch outhouse
        and the sod was as hard as stone,
Since a hole is just space, they laid rocks on the ground
        and left well-enough alone.

Sure, the outhouse is high, perched up on those flat slabs,
        and it's in the cow pasture to boot,
And the draft blows the paper right over your head
        'cause the wind through the rocks really hoots !
But they wired-in a heatlamp that toasts you above
        while your lower extremities chill.
With that red light it's comfy and risqué, I guess ;
        any more would have been overkill.

In the fall of the year, hunting season was on ;
        we'd been up playing games until late.
Nine-year-old Mark discovered his trip to the house-
        in-the-pasture-out-back couldn't wait.
Through the wind and the darkness, the boy made his run,
        did his job in the warmth of the lamp,
Pulled himself back together, yanked open the door
        and got set for his dash back to camp.

In the meantime, the bull in the pasture got curious :
        Who had invaded his space ?
And he stood just outside looking in through the door
        with red light on his eyes and his face.
Then we heard the boy howl, 'way above the wind noise,
        for his dad to come rescue his son.
He admitted, the fright could have made him "go" twice,
        but by then, all his business was done.
That was many years back and, though moved many times,
        that high outhouse accomplished its task,
But if you wonder why the bull pasture is dotted
        with extra-lush grass spots …don't ask !

THE FIGGERIN' MAN

There are men who drift through life
        whichever way the wind will blow.
There are men who follow, sheep-like,
        where the mindless flock will go.
There are men who seek out experts
        for a "proper" lifetime plan,
But not one of them can match
        the independent "figgerin' man".
Some will say it's simply laziness
        that motivates this guy.
Others say he's bored …
        compelled to give a new idea a try.
Some will say he's "just plain nuts",
        trying hard to stir up strife,
But you can't deny, the figgerin' man
        will add some spice to life.
If he's a rancher with some grass to grow,
        he's bound to play the odds
And survive by working some way
        to attract the moisture gods
And he's more surprised than anyone
        when rain begins to fall.
If it turns into a week-long soak,
        he's the happiest man of all !
After years of drought and snowless winters,
        one becomes concerned.
After months without a drop of rain,
        where's profit to be earned ?
So we should not be surprised
        if water thoughts go to his head.
Though he could lean back, content and wet,
        he's figgerin' rain instead !
How many times before
        he watched rainclouds approach … and pass,
And wondered how to keep his herd
        on short and withered grass.
Now, an inch and seven-tenths was dumped
        on his entire spread !
For each acre,
        twenty-seven thousand gallons he's ahead !

And on every section,
        nearly thirty million gallons fell :
"That's one hundred forty million gallons !"
        you can almost hear him yell.
Though his missus feels he could do
        some unfinished indoor chores,
At the moment, he's enjoying
        what's transpiring out-of-doors.
Just think if, by himself,
        he had to give his grass a drink !
That would take four lifetimes ...
        not a job you'd finish in a wink.
But, let's say he had a thousand gallon
        water tank to haul ;
That's one hundred forty thousand trips
        to spread it over all.
And where would he find a source pool,
        and a good-size pump to fill ?
(This could cause a war with all the other ranchers
        in the hills !)
Plus the cost in fuel and upkeep
        and the hours of time he spent,
Never mind the chance to strain his back,
        or have an accident.
At such a time you're not concerned
        with spills or evaporation
But other chores you need to do
        might deserve consideration.
So, for now, he's quite unburdened
        from the dryland rancher's care
As he watches, smiles and figgers ...
        feeling like a millionaire !
(Let's just hope the banker and the tax man
        don't stop by today.
For, if they believe his "figgers",
        they'll expect their yearly pay.)
It's a rare gift to defer the disappointments,
        stress and pain
And to thank the Lord for all the joy and magic ...
        in a rain.

Back in the Homestead Days, a lot of people didn't make it.
They starved out, sold out and moved out. Those who stayed,
whether "too broke" or "too dumb" to leave, did the best they
could with whatever was left behind.

HOMESTEAD RECYCLING

One winter morn, Pa stopped to say,
"I'll skid home Seitz's house today.
I'll build a barn with doors and wings
At a cost of hardly anything !"
He hitched his three teams side-by-side,
Reins-through-the-window on this ride.
They'd never pulled a house before ;
Two-story "sleds" are BIG, for sure !

Two miles downhill on ice and snow
With half the distance left to go
The horses spooked and ran away !
Control was lost ! No time to pray !
He could not jump to get away.
(This might turn out a "go-wrong" day !)
Hang on and ride 'er till the end ;
Thank God for witnesses and friends !

It rocked and reeled and flew through air.
The noise and fear were hard to bear.
They made a big loop through the yard.
Gramma was laughing awful hard !
Pa's wife and auntie were aghast …
This project might be Lester's Last !

He sawed the reins to slow them down
Till suddenly, they hit dry ground.
The horses stopped ! We heard Pa say,
"That's quite sufficient for today !"

The barn still stands right where they quit.
Pa saw no need to straighten it.
But laughter as the barn went past ?
"I never saw one move so fast !"

Introduction:
Cowboys don't like guardrails, much.
They get used to being alone
And they like the company.
They develop their own way of doing things
    …might not be the best way
    …might not be "right"
    …might not be "legal"
But it gets the job done.

This is a monologue …
That's like listening to one side of a telephone conversation.
In this case, only one guy had something important to say.

The man who said it was all cowboy.
Maybe you knew
    Slim Ragsdale

LAST RIDE PLUS ONE

Tell you what, boys. I been figurin' how we can get this done. It's easy. You all know this ain't no decent place for a man to go. Not for a feller like me, anyhow. And I can see this waitin' is kinda tough on you all, so here's the ticket.

You saddle up old Roanie, hitch up the horse trailer and leave it 'way back on the parkin' lot. I'll sneak out late, when it's quiet, mount up and head straight for the Bearpaws. I know them hills … spent most of my life ridin' that range. You give me a couple days … don't say nothin'. That oughta do 'er. Then you come out lookin'. Won't have no trouble findin' me … Roanie'll be close by. What can they do? Only me to blame.

Well you know I won't get no better! Been slidin' downhill steady. Shoulda stayed home.

We ain't got time to wait and see! Right now I got a choice. Few days, 'nother stroke, might not be able to climb in the saddle.

No, there ain't nothin' illegal about it! I can check myself out any time I want.

How much money we spendin' ever' day? And for what? Just do it! Don't think about it! Don't stew about it!

If I was still home, I'd take care of 'er myself … but I ain't. So I ask you boys. Ain't nothin' I wouldn't do myself.

I useta have friends woulda done 'er for me. I'da done 'er for them, too, I reckon.

I don't wanna be here! You know how I always been!
Just lemme do it my way! I oughta have a say! This is the last time I'll ask
you boys for anything. No more bossin'.
Well, I ain't gonna beg. Never done before … ain't gonna start now.
Okay, boys. I see how it is. At the last, a feller ain't got no choices …ain't
got no friends. Still ever' man for himself.
No, I don't blame you boys. You're the ones gotta live with it …not me.
Always knew … you want 'er done right, do 'er yourself. And when you
can't no more …   when you can't no more … I guess she don't get done.
Okay. Okay.

*   *   *   *

THE LITTLE COWBOY
True tale of a Boy and his Mother, in Four Episodes

The little cowboy was raised all alone
        on the Missouri River ranching scene.
For toys, he had horses and cows and guns,
        so his auntie feared he'd grow up mean,
And she counseled his mother. They got him a doll …
        celluloid with a rubber head.
But it didn't appeal to his feminine side ;
        it got fried on the cookstove instead.

Mother gave him a wagon … a little red wagon.
        Lots of kids have got the same.
But when you're alone and there's no one to pull,
        a red wagon is pretty tame.
So he roped the old cow, tied the rope to the tongue,
        settled in for a leisurely ride
And the plan went well till the cow looked around
        and saw where her harness was tied.
Then she went berserk, this gentle old cow,
        unaccustomed to panic or fits,
And she circled the snubbing post, doubling back,
        and smashed that red wagon to bits.

The folks were away so he borrowed his mom's
    single-shot twenty-two Remington.
Then he noticed the cow, the grazing milk cow.
    Shooting just past her nose should be fun.
Aiming fine, he let fly. She dropped to her knees !
    He was sure their old bossy was dead,
For his bullet had ricocheted off of the prairie
    and struck the cow square in the head.
For about the next week they could not milk that beast
    or get her to enter her stall.
As she passed the Carnation, mom tried to guess
    how that cow went plumb loco after all.

Then he fashioned a cannon from heavy-walled pipe,
    shooting sparkplugs with Cherry Bomb charge.
It was clamped in the vise on the workbench out back.
    With his cousin, he got a new urge.
If they aimed at the outhouse, and lay on the floor,
    and his mother would light the fuse,
They could learn how it feels to be shot at and missed !
    An experiment…all win, no lose !
So they hollered at mom in the kitchen, then hid.
    By and by she came out, lit the fire.
Boards were splintered, both sides, just over their heads !
    Mom helped raise their I.Q.s a bit higher !

So it went all her life with her supercharged son ;
    pretty much, an adventure-a-day.
But she never once "bumped him off" and,
    like all mothers, she loved him anyway.

ONE OF THOSE TAXING DAYS

We worked the bulls yesterday. I guess it went okay.
It's time to "bite-the-bullet" now and really earn our pay.
The corral looks like the target of a U.S. Army tank.
Them bulls is ornery buggers ; they're always on the crank.
But at least we're finally rid of the boss's cow-challenged dog !
Old Frozen Ears took him out like a runaway Unimog.

Well, okay. I drew the welder and Hank grabbed up the hammer.
('This cowboy-ism sucks,' I thought.
        'Where's the doggone glamour ?')
Hammerin' Hank was grumbling, "Where've all the pieces gone ?
Ain't enough to build an outhouse for a stunted leprechaun !"
But, I cranked up the welder after we got her kinda straight
And I commenced to weldin' on this so-called "bull-proof gate".

I had her propped up solid with the handle from the broom.
Then the shop cat brushed against it and …
        that's when I met with doom.
That bull gate landed on my lap just like a well-trained stripper
And it smashed the hot electrode … right up against my zipper.
Toxic fumes billowed from Fruit-of-the-Looms
        and singed hide from my gut.
I wrestled with my Wranglers … but my fly was welded shut.
I grabbed the fire extinguisher, rammed the nozzle down my pants,
Then I hopped around, doin' my version of a real unhappy dance.
At our First Aid station … (half pint of whiskey
        and a jug of scarlet oil,)
I dosed my insides with the hooch … and then applied the oil.

That's all I can bear to tell, but there's one thing that's gonna stop .
No more purrin' kitty cats when I'm workin' in the shop !

                                        Matt Eide

In preparation for the 2007 "Motherin' Up" gathering at
White Sulphur Springs, we were asked to do a poem around
the line: "She had her quirks, as all mothers do." I was having
trouble with it but my brother-in-law, a rancher from the Sweetgrass
Hills and a man of few words, said, "It's easy."

LOST CALF

She had her quirks, as all mothers do ;
      She ran around the pasture goin' "Moo, Moo, Moo !"

"That's it ?" I asked.
"Yep," he said.

MY CHICKENS

The Chicken is a wondrous creature any way you take it,
Particularly if you boil, fry, barbecue or bake it.
And O ! The joy of chicken noodle soup by cup or bowl
Plus eggs ten ways, or pickled, so you have to eat them whole.
There's chicken liver dumpling soup ; there's chicken fricassee ;
There's chicken cacciatore for a taste of Italy.
For culinary change-of-pace the chicken has no equal …
More toothsome taste delights that leave one yearning for a sequel.
But, looking back at all the things I've written, thought or said,
My preference is clear : I most enjoy my chickens … dead.

MARCH COLD SPELL

It's lucky for some folks I know who play with cows and calfs
That someone thinks enough of them to send them poems for laughs
So when they're basking by the stall and waiting for some action,
There's ART to work the mind and supplement the main attraction.
Of course I'm happy to provide those folks with mental candy.
At calving time the hours are long ; diversion comes in handy.
But while they wait and lounge around that cozy polebarn shelter
At twenty, twenty-five below with livestock helter-skelter
And ice and snow outside the door all set to freeze the profits
With music of the wind a-howling 'round the eaves and soffits,
I hope they give a thought to how the lonely poet suffers ...
Blank page and pen, in easy chair, by stove, like many duffers.
The perfect word, the clever rhyme, the meter flowing freely,
The meaning deep, precise ... range of emotion, soft to steely,
The agony of finding words so right but never rhyming,
The heartache caused by lines unfit for rhythm and for timing,
All these and more, once overcome, the poet suffers gladly
To light his reader's face and heart with happiness ... yet, sadly
The artist can not live alone, for feedback is so needful,
And those who view his work should darnwell listen and be heedful !
In conversation, give-and-take is what I think is swell.
Do folks appreciate this stuff ? Sometimes it's hard to tell.
So tell him ! Whistle, stomp or hoot or clap, or write a letter.
He'll have to try, and come again ... and next time, do it better.

MAMA ZANE

Let's hear it for the Powell kid who went the "extra mile"
To mother-up his calves and cows in true Montana Style.
He trailed his pairs along the crick in very early spring.
He wore his parka, longjohns, mitts, boots, chaps and everything.
They trailed along till suddenly, the scene was not so nice.
One little calf was floating down the crick among the ice !
He couldn't let his new calf drown and hear its mama bawl.
With motherly abandon, RESCUE overshadowed all !
While shedding clothes, he ran and dived into that icy stream.
(No witness but the cows and horse to hear him cuss and scream.)
He fought his way across and grabbed that shaking, soggy mass,
Then fought back, just in time to keep from freezing off his ... legs.
He felt a little like a cow, fierce guardian of her young,
As he went to re-unite the pair. (Where did that calf belong ?)
A mother's love sustained him while he saw and acted quick,
But the calf had come from the neighbor's herd ...
From the other side of the crick.

*   *   *   *

PHEW = PeeYOO !

I climbed up in the tractor cab to feed the calves and cows.
My dog jumped in ; he guards the gate, the way I taught him how.
I closed the door and noticed something pungent in the air.
I said, "You rolled in something dead..and recent..who knows where!"
I left him at the haylot gate, expecting freer breathing
But as I worked, I noticed, something rotten was still seething.
With recent snow, my Herefords all had suffered sunburned bags;
They kicked their sucking calves away. I couldn't blame those hags.
I ran them in the chute to milk and treat and let calves suck,
A job that soaked my coveralls with several kinds of "Yuck".
Too cold to leave them off ; too busy calving yet to wash,
I thought about that awful stench and mumbled, "Ohmygosh !"
It's 'way past laundry time, and I owe an apology.
"I'm sorry, dog. Jump up. The only stinker here ... is me !"

PINTO

For years, I sought a pickup nice enough to go to church.
I drove old junkers, but continued to pursue the search.
And then one day, out of the blue, I found a fancy rig.
(I hesitate to haul a load that's dirty, rough or big.)
It's bright and shiny over-all with just a couple "blems".
Not perfect, but compared to what I had, one of the "gems".
I park it off the street, close to the corner of our lot
Which, up till now, has been a safe and unobtrusive spot.
And then my neighbor, bless his heart, set up a feeder station
For all the homeless birds in town, (or possibly, the nation !)
They flock and fight and peck and gorge and fly into my tree
To do their "Number One" and "Two" ..(Do birds do "Number Three?)
Some young nutritionist should study sidewalk, truck and street.
Digestion, many times, I fear, is somewhat incomplete.
They must have put more flaxseed in their "perfect birdseed blend";
My windows show, those birds got diarrhea in the end.
So now I have a Pinto Pickup ... (Some folks call it "Paint"),
But you and I both know that "paint" is one thing that it ain't !
At least he's not yet feeding eagles, seagulls, geese and ducks.
I guess bird-love just makes a target of our cars and trucks.
To hide my shameful pickup ... (well, you KNOW how people talk !)
Next time I up and go to church, I guess I might/could walk

*　　　　*　　　　*　　　　*　　　　*

SECOND BEST

My old watchdog grins and shows a set of teeth that snap and sparkle
But, of course, she can't compete and tear off chunks the way a shark'll ;
Still, I don't believe I'll trade my trusty hound dog for a "fish"
For she works well on dry land, comes back, and fetches when I wish
And really, if her dentures aren't enough to scare you off, her bark'll.

81

THE RIGHT STUFF

He howled, first time his hat blew off and landed in the mud.
At brandin', it took on a little green, a little blood.
He cussed the dog that chewed the hole right up there by the crease.
By summer's end the hatband looked like it was soaked in grease,
Through rain and fire-fightin', stompin', hazin', "bob-wire" fence,
His old hat needed fixin', though it didn't make much sense,
But it had been a good old hat; he'd hate to let it go.
He asked his daddy how to keep the brim from droopin' so.

Old Dad is quite a cowboy, wise in ways that work out west.
He recommended duct tape for repairs that last the best.
That hat has plenty character from battles lost and won.
(Replacement time was here. We did what needed to be done.)
We sent our "smokin' miles" to get his brand-new Stetson lid,
A spiffy 5-X beaver ... makes a manly-lookin' kid !
He seemed to have a little strut when wearin' it around
At weddings, funerals and such, or just a trip to town.

His friends, the ones who matter most, began to call him "Dude".
The truth can hurt. (Of course, they didn't have to be so rude.)
I guess he made an attitude adjustment on himself.
The Stetson went back in the box ; it's waitin' on the shelf.
He must have thought about it ... "showin' off" or "fittin' in".
Among his friends he wears his beat-up hat and sports a grin.
He saves the Stetson just for "nice".
            I asked him why.
                    He said,
"Dad says a cowboy's Bona Fide
            with duct tape on his head."

THEY NEVER LEARN

It's a ripping of a canvas; it's a nail upon a slate;
It's the protest of the hinges on a long-neglected gate.
It's the screeching of a buzz saw when it hits a nasty knot.
Such a sound, once heard, is hated, and will never be forgot.
It's a common cause for guilty cussing, every time it's done;
Instant shock, surprise and recognition, all rolled into one.
You would think, once taught, he'd learn
      and never do it any more,
When the tomcat gets his tail caught,
      sneakin' through the kitchen door.

SORRY , WRONG NUMBER

The wife and I had gone to town. We'd be gone overnight.
We left our teenage son at home,
       keeping an eye on the place.
But teens are unpredictable ... (I once was one myself.)
Until we started home, I thought I'd phone
       and just "touch base".

I punched my cellphone ; surely he'd be close enough to hear,
But all I got was "busy signal" .
       Okay ... call again.
I waited, but my second call result was just the same.
(He surely wouldn't call his friends
       to drink my stash of beer ?!)

Another call ... another busy signal ... what the heck ?
If he was hurt, or raising cain,
       he'd "catch it in the neck" !
He might have left it off the hook in case the folks should call
While he and all his buddies
       wrecked the house and had a ball !

And then the wife ... (they have a way of cutting to the quick,)
So calm and sweetly asked,
       "What number are you calling, dear ?"
Instead of home, I'd called my cell ... and it's been busy here.
I'll take this number off this menu .
       That should do the trick !

THE ROAD HOME

I think I'd be happy as happy could be
      If I lived on a road that was named after me
And I wouldn't mind sharing with neighbor or friend
      But I think I'd want my place to be at the end
Or at least, pretty close. If I got company
      They'd remember it's me they were coming to see.
If I got drunk or goofy and started to roam
      I'd just call 9-1-1 for directions to home
And if Alzheimer's made me forget at the end
      There would always be one place they'd know who I'd been.
When my time was used up and I laid down my load
      I would hope I could rest at the end of my road.

SWEETGRASS HILLS SPRING

I remember mid-April of twenty-ought-eight
      When it came on brandin' time.
It came in like a lamb, dry and sunny and warm,
      work conditions mighty fine.
I invited my crew. We'd get started at ten.
      The wife prepared quite a feed
Plus a little bit extra ...
      (we always attract a few more cowpokes than we need.)
About then we heard weathercasters up North ...
      (well, you know how Canadians are,)
"Heavy snow, wind and cold are headed this way,
      who knows how soon, how long or how far ?"
So I kept a sharp eye on the top of Gold Butte.
      when the clouds start driftin' our way ...
Sure enough, there was nastiness crossin' the line,
      and it didn't mean "Have a nice day !"
I got word to my crew, "Boys, at sunup we ride.
      Let's cinch up, mount up and slap leather.
When we're done we can party. For now, do your best.
      Keep this brandin' ahead of the weather."
So we slipped and we slid and we rolled in the mud ;
      chilly wind blew burnt hair stink away.
When we sat down to eat, Ol' Man Winter was back
      and our wranglers had not much to say.
Soon they drifted on home. Not too many took seconds.
      Our cook was in kind of a pique.
She prepared enough vittles for twenty more cowboys.
      We'll be eating leftovers all week !
Only thing we can hope : if the in-laws drop by
      when they hear that the brandin' is done,
(They're not fussy as long as there's plenty of grub.
      They rank cowboy food second-to-none !)
We can feed 'em up good with the stuff we have left
      ... make some points while we clean up this mess.
If they think we went overboard makin' 'em welcome,
      who can blame us if we don't confess ?

TAKING STOCK

When we do double-takes at some cowboy's mistakes
    With his horse, with his tack, with his tools,
And we laugh and have fun when that sonofagun
    Just ignores all the laws and the rules.
When he doctors himself with some cure off the shelf
    And he don't have much use for a clock,
With the sun, up at dawn ; work till dark when it's gone ...
    One more day with the hay and the stock.
He's been known to make deals on land, livestock or wheels
    And to "sign" with a handshake or nod.
And he'll see it gets done, tho' it might not be fun,
    (Barrin' late intervention by God.)
While he's out fixin' fence, he might try to make sense
    Of the jungle we live in today.
And his money's to spend or to lend to a friend ...
    He'll most likely be paid back some way.
Well, that's just how he is and it's nobody's biz'
    And we sure wouldn't change him ... No Way !
And we thank God above who can show enough love
    That the cowboy survives yet today
While there's still time and space, far beyond the rat race,
    Where we need him and want him to be
And he's sure of his place in the whole human race
    With his life, independent and free.

Well, it ain't the Frontier, but it often feels near
    When you're 'way out and workin' alone
And you'd best use your head or you could wake up dead
    From a fall or a cut or broke bone.
It's a life plenty rough and the work's always tough
    And you never match hours with pay,
And it's easy to curse but you might have had worse ;
    It's familiar ... the old cowboy way.
And you treasure the way, sometimes at end-of-day,
    You take stock of the blessings you've got
And you'd rather, by far, be the man that you are
    Than some strange imitation you're not.

But, what I meant to say 'fore I plumb strayed away
       Is ... this humor we call "Cowboy Poem"
Is a neighborly thing, though it might bite and sting
       When the point of it finally hits home.
But we never laugh AT him ... we always laugh WITH him
       Though sometimes he don't see the joke
Till we buy him a drink and allow him to think
       And cool off with a chew or a smoke.

Now, I guess we all know, cowboys ain't much for show,
       And there's mighty few famous or rich,
But I've stated their case and I doubt they'll trade place
       With some "citified" guy-who-would-switch !

WALT AND ERNIE – A Shocking Tale

Walter never cared for fencing …
        quite a job in rocky ground.
Now and then he used some dynamite
        to dig the corner holes
And, although he got a kick
        from setting off that blast and sound,
He just LOVED electric fence with light, thin wire
        and short push poles.
In a jiffy he could set a fence
        of any size and shape,
Anywhere and any time.
        Like magic, cows and bulls behaved !
Well I GUESS it made his neighbor, Ernie,
        listen-up and gape
When he saw how easy Walt's life was
        and how much time he saved.
Being cautious, Ernie didn't buy,
        but borrowed, just to try it
And it BIT him, so he NEVER bought !
        (He hated to get zapped.)
His electric fence love/hate relationship …
        none would deny it,
For, if you don't OWN it,
        you blame someone else for your mishaps !

Walt and Ernie had to bale,
        but was it dry enough quite yet ?
Walt's bib overalls had plenty room
        and baggy, shock-proof crotch.
Ernie wore Levis and belt
        for leaner, meaner silhouette.
When they reached THE FENCE,
        Walt stepped across, there was no need to watch,
And he pinched the insulator,
        slid the wire down to the ground :
(He was thinking of his neighbor …
        let ol' Ernie stroll across.)
And he turned to look for Ernie
        when he heard that awful sound.
In a flash, this perfect haying day
        looked more like … Total Loss !

In the dewy grass lay Ernie,
  spread as flat as any toad,
Hot "weed-burner" wire across his back ...
  he had not quite crawled under !
He was sure Walt meant to send him
  to his heavenly abode,
And his commentary filled with sulfur, smoke,
  brimstone and thunder.
(Ernie knew three-, four-, five-letter words
  and used them fast and well.)
Questioned Walt's intentions, ancestry,
  background and future, too ...
Spoke with heart-felt force and feeling
  and as clear as any bell ...
Made it clear , Walt's "helpful act"
  was not a friendly thing to do.

Quick-as-a-wink,
  Walt saved his near-electrocuted neighbor,
Saw he'd made a small mistake
  but knew he didn't dare to laugh,
Vaguely wondered who he might hire now
  for help-with-haying labor ?
Ernie was insulted ... branded ...prone
  and bawling like a calf!

THE WOODGATE AFFAIR

Well, I cut my wood in little chunks
    and pile it in a shelter
Where I keep it dry till winter.
    (Wife would like her house to swelter.)
Then I pull the prop and lower the gate
    and haul wood to the kitchen
And it keeps us cozy till it's gone
    and wife begins to screechin'
Then I raise the gate and set the prop
    and saw till overflowin'
So, week after week, month after month,
    I keep the woodpile goin'.

Every now and then I find a board or plank
    that's somethin' fancy
And I set it off to save
    until my "buildin' urge" gets antsy
So, from time to time,
    I get a stock of lumber that's appallin'
And, you guessed it,
    that would be the time the brother-in-law comes callin'.

Well, this time he said
    he sold a cow and calf to get some money
And to hear him justify
    his "truck-and-trailer-trip" is funny
But as long as he's got haulin' space
    and I've got extra lumber,
Could I spare a thousand feet or so
    of random size and number ?

Since he brought us spuds and pickles
    and arrived in time for dinner,
It's a little hard to boot him out
    like any bum or sinner
So we feed him up ... him and his wife ...
    and after lunch they wonder,
Could we lend a hand to load him up ? ...
    our own free boards, By Thunder !

Just to get him gone, we pack the planks.
　　　　His smile grows wide and bigger
And, I'll-go-to-heck,
　　　　if he don't pull his pencil out and figure
Dollar value of HIS boards ...
　　　　subtract a hundred for nail-pullin' !
(I just gotta walk away
　　　　and give my temper time for coolin')
While I'm gone,
　　　　my storage box and meat saw manage to get loaded.
Then when I return,
　　　　the whole shebang has left and down-the-roaded !

When I take a walk through my backyard
　　　　that I keep neat and spiffy,
Everywhere, there's empty space,
　　　　but I spot trouble in a jiffy.
All my firewood tumbled down
　　　　because the gate was left to drop !
Brother-in-law has struck again,
　　　　and even stole my woodgate prop !

YIPPEE TI YI OW!

Right above the kitchen window,
        close beside the kitchen door,
Yellow Jackets started up a nest.
        (That's what house eaves are for.)
And the Missus told the Mister,
        "NOW is when you ought to act.
Do not dawdle
        till the kids and I are finally attacked !"
But the warm spring winds, green grass and flowers,
        all new signs of life,
Calves and chores and optimism ...
        sometimes, you ignore the wife,
And it wasn't long till she got stung
        and marked it with a shout.
Then he knew the time had come
        to move the Yellow Jackets out.

So he took control and set his jaw and said,
        "This, too, shall pass !"
And he splashed their little start-up nest
        with stinky tractor gas.
Several applications later, he declared,
        "This ain't the ticket.
It WOULD work if I got close enough
        and knew just where to stick it !"

Was it Heloise
        or just the neighbor giving good advice ?
"Use your fire extinguisher
        and you won't have to spray 'em twice !"
He had never said a fire man
        was the kind he'd like to be
But he holstered his extinguisher ...
        All Purpose, A-B-C".
WHOOSH ! He shot...and saw them come
        ...and ran for safety in his home.
Then it's "back door only", and he thought,
        'I should've sprayed with FOAM'.
For two, three days, they'd fly
        and leave a vapor trail of powder

Which makes them MAD, not sick or slow,
          and doesn't make them louder,
But it makes some pretty patterns in the air,
          sundown or dawn.
Still, it doesn't show you where the ARE,
          but where they've been and gone.

"I could take a skinny pole
          and jab 'em down and get away.
They might be upset awhile,
          but then I bet they wouldn't stay."
Just imagine, jousting with a bee !
          It simply makes no sense
For, like buffalo, they have no rules
          and don't respect a fence.
Just like Don Quixote
          or a knight from Arthur's Camelot,
He hoisted lance and mounted up,
          straight for the trouble spot.
Taking pity on his horse, TwoDot,
          he opted for the pickup.
Since it has a sunroof,
          it might give advantage in the sneak-up.
He could drive up close, stand up
          and poke the hive down with the pole.
Poor planning here, he guessed :
          his "lance" stuck out the open hole.
It must have looked suspicious
          as he rumbled toward their nest.
The bees responded quickly,
          they did not remain at rest,
And they found the open sunroof hole
          and started flying in
And the speed of his departure ?
          It was practically a sin !

Every cowboy has a limit
          when there's no more he can do.
(In abrupt retreat,
          his "steed" backed over their new barbecue !)
"Fair play" was out !
          the bees had lost their chance to leave with honor !
Every blasted, blinkin', buzzin'

Yellow Jacked was a goner !
"We'll resort to deadly chemicals
          to help resolve our plight !
Ah, but how do we get close enough ?
          We have to plan this right !"
So we see six feet of cowboy
          stretched across the kitchen sink
Leaning out the window, on his back.
          "Spray straight, before you blink !"
"Here now, Missus !
          Drag me in and slam the window ! Watch the head !"
Oops ! One bee got in ... and buzzed ...
          and had a tailspin ... and fell dead.

He's a man of honor
          and he loves the challenge of Fair Chase,
But when bees, and wife, start buzzing ...
          modern science has its place.

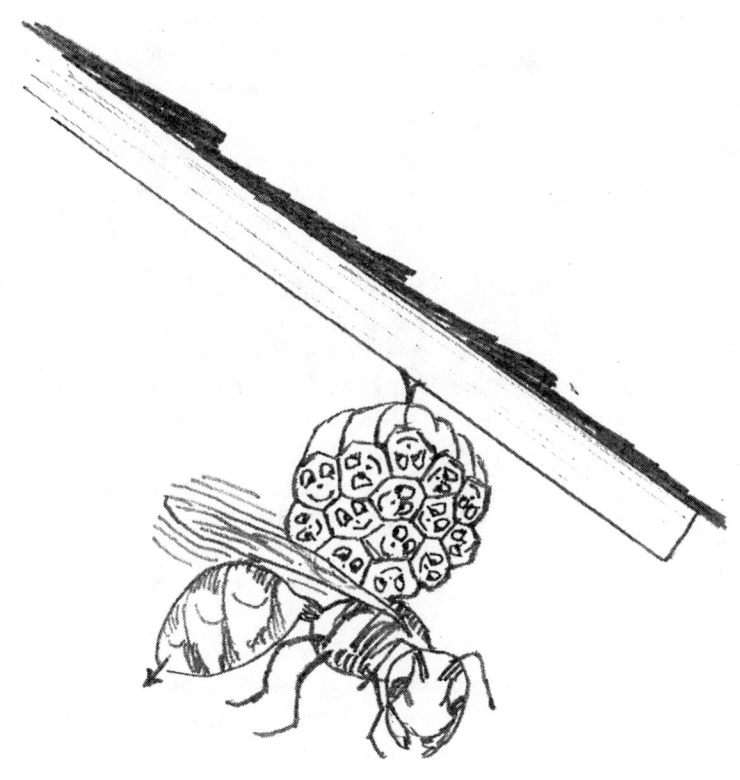

YOU JUST NEVER KNOW

"You have got to get rid of that mean Guernsey bull",
    said the partner of most of his life.
"I'm afraid if you don't, and he ever gets loose,
    you will find yourself minus one wife !
He hates me. He'll "take" me, I've told you before.
    He has blood in his eye, I can see !
And I'd rather not end up like old Crazy Bill,
    mashed to mush in the crotch of a tree !"

Pa valued Ma's judgment, he knew she was right,
    but just now he was somewhat distracted.
Other jobs must be finished. He postponed the call,
    though he knew it was time that he acted.
So he spent the whole morning with tractor, afield,
    and he finished a little bit late.
He was already planning his afternoon work
    …but at noon mealtime, cooks hate to wait !

As he "popped" up the trail on his John Deere
he thought,
    "This is how life's intended to be !"
Everything in its place as he neared the hillcrest :
    "There's the barn, the windmill, the pine tree,
And the bull on his hind legs, dancing around,
    And my wife sitting on the fence post !"
It was just such a moment that makes one reflect,
    Which behavior surprises the most ?

First Pa rescued his wife, perching meadow lark style,
    Then he turned back to deal with the bull.
But with great indignation, the bull shambled off.
    Ma reported the details in full.
She had walked out to see what had kept Pa so long,
    Past the bull in the pasture nearby,
And her skirt caught the breeze like a matador's cape
    And the bull didn't stop to ask why.

He pawed and he snorted, he bellowed, he charged,
    Seeing only his target ahead,
And Ma ran for the only safe haven around :
    Fence-sitting is better than dead !
And the bull, in his haste, hit Pa's "weed burner" fence
    The electric wire caught in his "choppers",
And he rose up to paw at the fire in his mouth,
    Unconcerned with behavior improper.

Not an hour went by till Pa called the sale barn
    And the bull was shipped off right away.
As the sunset came down and Pa finished the chores,
    He'd accomplished a lot in one day.
To his neighbors he said, "I knew something was wrong
    Just as soon as I heard that bull roar
At my wife on the cornerpost, 'cause neither one
    Ever acted so crazy before !"

CHAPTER FOUR

SMORGASBORD

*　　*　　*　　*　　*

These are poems that do not fit into another category. Some were written for effect, to see how they would bounce off an audience. Others were exercises to accomplish a particular goal. Still others were written just for fun.

FLUSHED WITH SUCCESS

The flusher in the men's room has an interesting quirk :
The "go" is fine ; the "automatic stop" won't always work.
It's not the flusher on the floor ; it's that one on the wall.
By now, it's trained our office staff, inspectors, guests and all.
It misfires only sometimes, and at last, it picked on Jim.
It kept on "frantic flushing" and it sprayed a bit on him.
Not knowing how to shut it off, he asked the boss for aid.
(He knew what water service costs,
        and Jim was quite dismayed.)

"It's nothing new," the boss replied. "To get it to un-stick,
Just biff it with your hand, right here, and give a hefty lick."
So after that, Big Jim would biff, and biff with quite a will.
Sometimes it took 3, 4 good shots
        to make that flush valve still.
And then one day, all innocent, he biffed the pipe in two
And instantly, Jim learned that one must never overdo.
Water, water everywhere, but not to drink or wash !
Big Jim was soaked ! In full retreat, he burbled, "Ohmygosh !"

The plumber came, replaced the pipe, we didn't give him lip.
He said, "Don't break it off ! Just give the handle-thing a "flip".
The flusher valve is still the same. We flip it as before.
We opted not to change it, but don't biff it anymore.
Big Jim has since decided to retire. We wished him well.
His yarn is now public domain for anyone to tell.

Just for fun, during April Poetry Month, I wrote the following and
sent it off to the newspaper.

APRIL FANTASY

I ought to rhyme something for Poetry Month
      As April so aptly is named.
I bet if some publisher liked it a lot
      I'd be well-paid and widely acclaimed,
And when I got famous, they'd want me to star
      In movies, recordings and books.
They'd beg for my autograph, reach for my hand
      And throw oodles of envious looks.
I'd live in a mansion, or maybe a castle …
      Retire, so rich, I would stink !
I'd pay someone else to do everything for me …
      Write poems, give speeches, and think !
So, here's to my future : I might "have it all",
      Though I'd be content with just half,
Or even a quarter, and possibly less,
      For my readers to get a good laugh.

     *   *   *   *

The newspaper printed my poem … minus one whole line.
I wrote a second poem after discovering that April is also
Humor Month. Possibly, the editor was just "being funny".

THE LAFF'S ON US

I know now why they did it, and it's pretty funny, too,
For April "Humor Month" rates high with our Journal-istic crew.
When I sent a funny poem to entertain our local wits,
April 9 they put it on A-5 … right close to the obits.
We've all tried dancing to a band that drops a beat or two,
And a deck that's short a few cards makes the dealer fret and stew,
And a load that's shy a couple bricks can make contractors bawl,
But an eight-line poem that's lost one line don't make no sense at all!
Undaunted, I will try again to give you folks a snicker,
But it's possible the radio would be a little quicker.

BIGGER AND BETTER

I always liked a pencil
        till they made me use a pen.
When I squawked, they told me firmly,
        "This is NOW and that was THEN."
I learned to use a pen :
        the leaky, sketchy, smooth and rough.
(I hate 'erasable",
        and black or blue are good enough.)
I got so good,
        I did my crossword puzzles all in ink,
And then somebody said,
        "You need a typewriter, I think.
For your formal presentations,
        you can't do longhand or print."
So I learned to type
        to show I'm smart enough to take a hint.
Many years I used the manual,
        and then electric, too,
Till the boss said,
        "Now it's time to work with something really new."
We installed the big computer :
        much more work and really fast,
Hooked up the internet and fax
        to solve our problems of the past.
Now it's virus, worm, re-program,
        power surge, brownout and blip,
Update codes, spam screening, ROM and RAM
        and discs that flop and flip.
We can boast of world-wide access,
        endless info with a click,
But now, have we traded "life" for "electronic",
        vast and quick ?
I prefer to sit out by a tree
        or at my kitchen table
To visit, work or think and write,
        to what extent I'm able.
For I miss the robin singing
        in the branches overhead,
Neighbor kids who pause to hear me read

what funny stuff I said.
I enjoy the old cat making figure eights
       around my feet,
Puzzled looks and waves from passers-by
       have always been a treat.
And I miss the hands-on process,
       working thoughts onto a page,
Crossing out and rearranging ...
       personal control of change.
So I sit outdoors and scribble,
       basic pencil in my hand.
Rise up, pencil-pushing dinosaurs !
       It's time to make a stand !

SHORTIES

DYSLEXIC

They say I have "dyslexic mouth" ...
    It's hard for me to know,
        So, if I greet you with "O Hell",
          I likely mean "Hello".

*   *   *   *   *   *   *

RESPECT

When you get no respect for awhile,
And you show signs of strain in your   smile,
Let me hasten to mention,
Some adverse attention
Beats being ignored, by a mile !

COUNT ON ME

I said I would, and so I will, but darned if I know why.
It's never been a crisis ; no one feared to live or die.
And, almost always, there are lots of other things to do
For wife or kids or friends or work or sometimes, for me, too.
My problem is, I can't say "No" when someone is in need
Because they're sure I am the only one to do the deed.
They sing my praise, for I am such a handy guy to know
And, though refusal was my goal, some voice says,
      "...told you so !"

*   *   *   *   *   *   *

Someone called the poet, Fred Liese, "beloved" and "normal".
Those who knew him rose up in protest.

DON'T SAY IT'S SO
EVEN IF IT'S SO

When I was but a young man,
I heard a wise man say,
"To compliment a cowboy
Is to throw your breath away.
He'll scold and scoff and snicker
And say you're "full of it".
He'll shower insults on your head
And that's the best you'll get.

When I was still a young man,
I learned to curb my tongue.
Not greet with "Sir" or "Mister"
To cowboys old or young.
I'd shake their hand or nod or wink
At the awesome things they'd do
And I'm getting to be an old man
So I know it's pretty much true.

EFFICIENCY STUDY

The people at the clinic handed me a questionnaire.
I guess they want to know how well
    the system's working there.
It's all about when you came in and when you saw the Doc.
They furnish pen and clipboard and a five-buck K-Mart clock.
The questions probe where-all you went
      and how much time you stayed
And did their finance office make arrangements to be paid.
I filled in all the blanks that were related to my case
But then I had to write "N. A." in every other space.
I only needed someone there to take my stitches out.
The Doc worked on my chart ;
    nurse one and two bustled about.
I must have healed too fast.
    The thread had pulled in awful tight
And, though they yanked and tweaked,
    that little loop stayed out-of-sight.
"We need a sharper scissor, bigger tweezer, better light !"
Both Doc and nurse "had at it" and it put up quite a fight.
They saw me mark my sheet.
    Quick visits always take too long.
They tried to get me gone while taking care to "do no wrong".
At last they gave a snip and rip. That little stitch pulled free.
We joked about the semi-mortal damage done to me.
No stitches this time ; simple salve and band-aid did the trick.
They wished me well and shooed me
    to the lobby double-quick.
I wouldn't be surprised to learn they dropped my survey sheet
In that "round file" located by the office lady's feet.
Now, if you find yourself a random clinic survey guest,
Be brief, leave clipboard, clock and pen
    with the lady at the desk.

One day at the supermarket, all I wanted was a jug of milk.
But I looked up. Never look up when all you want is a jug
of milk. Stacked on the dairy cooler were six cartons as big
as Coleman lanterns. They were not Coleman lanterns.
They were electric indoor windchimes. There's a little fan
in the base that jiggles the chimes and makes soothing sounds.
Many residents of the windy HiLine have never needed such
an appliance. Some do, I guess.

ENVIRASCAPE ELECTRIC INDOOR WINDCHIME

I just beheld the latest toy ...
        as cool as Fonzie Winkler,
And now I can't go on
        without the AC/DC Tinkler !
It will not purify your air
        or add some perfume to it.
And if you want a cooling breeze,
        this outfit can not do it.

It can not sharpen pencils
        and it's not a night light, either.
If you want music or the news,
        this rig can furnish neither.
You say you go for action toys ?
        Go out and watch your sprinkler.
Because, as I declared before,
        this thing is just a tinkler.

The simulated wind
        that breaks across the chimes so clinky
Is better than the real thing,
        and never, ever stinky.
It won't fight colds or allergies,
        nor stop gas pains or wrinkles.
· I told you once or twice before,
        this is the toy that tinkles.

Be first to thrill your friends,
        whose faces into smiles will crinkle.
There's nothing so rejuvenating
        as a quiet tinkle.

It might not calm as quickly
        as a stiff two-fingered drink'll.
No matter. Find a private nook
        and do a little tinkle.

Renew, refresh,
        as from the tranquil fount of sound you're drinking.
For calming minds and soothing souls,
        there's nothing like some tinking.
Remember bedtimes,
        when your mom would read "Wee Willie Winkle"?
She'd say, "You never rest your best
        until you've had your tinkle".

FREE REIN

It behooves a guide of youngsters to maintain an open mind,
            To accept the little buggers where they're at.
Once assignment is requested, fertile minds are free to roam,
            Even when they mix the fire with the fat.

Like the ripples from a skipping stone, or bouncing of a ball,
            Youthful minds can harvest gold from hill or dale.
Half the job of education is in knowing where to look.
            Sometimes, borrowed thoughts
                        from older minds prevail.

Rest assured, sweet girls can squash a bug
                        or cuss like sailors, too ;
            Be advised, tough boys have gentle sides as well.
We must look at every side of us to find out who we are.
            ART is what we reach inside ourselves to tell.

Whether story, poem or picture or a carving on a wall,
            Or a song or tune or just a job well-done,
Any time we are creative and can call a work our own,
            That's the time when we are truly "having fun".

Let the chips fly from the axe ! Let the dust fly from the saw !
            Let them follow butterflies from bud to bloom !
While their minds are fresh and limber,
                        let them exercise each part.
            Soon enough, free minds are given little room.

Be it naughty, dumb or silly, be it shocking, gross or smart,
            If the kid has worked it over till it's good,
If the work is true and honest, if it simmered in the heart,
            Would I take it for a grade ? Damright I would !

THE LAST TO GO

Last week, at my mirror, I saw signs of trouble ...
    A chilling reality sight.
While I truly regret bursting anyone's bubble,
    Perhaps you could share in my fright.
The hairs in my nostrils are fading to white
    And it leaves me a little bit blue.
Since my hair everywhere has endured the same plight
    There is not a whole lot I can do,
For I fear it's a stage, as a sign of my age,
    And I'm not any longer a kid,
So I'll go sniff a rose as reward for my nose,
    Holding out for as long as it did.
Tiny moments of joy satisfy spirit-hunger ...
    All five senses recall "where" and "when" ...
And although they won't render us one minute
    younger,
They remind us how happy we've been.

In March, 2007, I surveyed Glasgow's interest in cowboy poetry.
I learned about Jim Nelson, poet, performer, and author of two
books, which I eventually acquired, thanks to Shirley Nelson.
With Doris Ozark of the Valley Ridge Runners Saddle Club,
we staged the First Annual Jim Nelson Memorial Gathering on
Halloween, attended by over 100 people.

JIM

It's kinda nice, havin' a friend in case yer feelin' tough.
Seems like, now that I'm "gettin' on", I never have enough
So when another chance came up, I didn't hesitate.
(There's times when you just can't afford time to procrastinate.)
I met a cowboy just last week ...went by the handle, "Jim".
A frisky sort of feller, full of life right to the brim
And that was curious
        because his wife and friends all said,
"You woulda loved ol' Jim, I bet,
        except he's six months dead."
So when I say we met,
        I never grabbed his hand and shook
I got to know him pretty well
        by readin' in his book.
There's lots of fellers go through life
        and leave no map or track.
I reckon they was pretty sure
        they wasn't comin' back.
But Jim, he done 'er different.
        He loved the life he lived
And in this world of give-and-take,
        he leaned hard towards the "give".
He didn't just tell best-of-times ...
        he told his troubles, too
So even when he had a wreck,
        the real Jim showed through
And, day or night, he'd write his life,
        at rest or doin' chores.
When inspiration hit, he'd scribble verse
        on walls and doors.
I don't believe he meant to teach
        by what he had to say.
I reckon all he wanted
        was to show he'd passed this way

Like travelers in days of old
      when men would mark their trail
To show the many things they tried in life ...
      succeed or fail.
I met his wife. She smiled and talked
      of how they got along.
They done their best, they raised their kids,
      they taught 'em right from wrong.
But I could tell ... I seen her eyes ...
      it warn't no easy job.
On silky skin and shiny curls,
      this prairie life "plays hob".
But, they was partnered-up;
      they made adjustments on the way.
Like him, her life is tied up
      in their western exposé.
I know now why his friends' eyes shone
      when I inquired for Jim.
He put some sunshine in their lives ;
      they kept that part of him.

Yep, Jim is gone, but he'll keep givin' in his homely way.
His life, and love, are in his book. Go visit him some day.

MOCCASIN BLUES

My moccasins have rubber soles. From innertubes they're made.
A truck tube seems to work the best. It's thicker by a "shade".
The rubber gives a non-slip grip, far longer life than leather,
And helps to keep my toesies dry in snow or rainy weather.

I take my pattern, slap it down and cut the tube around it.
(Remember : glue the bumpy side.
 Adhesion's best, I've found it.)
Contact cement still works the best ... both sides,
 and wait till tacky.
(Sit back and smoke, or sip a beer,
or chew Red Man tobacky.)
Retreaded mocs will last for years.
They're cheap, they're neat, they're snappy,
And all you do ? You just re-glue whenever they get "flappy"!

Why, just today I saw my toe was leaking out and dusty.
I set about to fix my mocs, so comfy, cool and trusty.
A little hole I overlooked. I hadn't time to worry.
I glued it up and put it on. (It seldom pays to hurry.)

There is a certain feeling, like a bug caught in the honey.
You laugh about it now, but at the time, it wasn't funny.
Like when you're sweaty and your skin
 and clothing stick together,
Or superglue your fingers, or lick iron in frigid weather,
Or lay banana peeling on the back of pussycat ...
A trapped and stupid feeling ... and my foot felt just like that .

I think the skin can change its outer cells in seven days.
Till then, my moc and I will stick together. Happy Days

NEARLY NOT

They say he never found himself,
      No lifestyle ever clicked.
He always seemed a half-turn off
      Whatever path he picked.

He did not soar to ecstasy
      Nor sink to dark despair.
A man of beige, he lived his life
      As if he couldn't care.

Amid the thrills of sight and sound
      And smell and taste and touch,
He played his roles but, all in all,
      They didn't matter much.

At last he shuffled off,
      Maybe to heaven ... maybe hell.
With no more practice than he had,
      Who knows if he could tell ?

ILLUSION

The course of a life is not easy to chart.
There are changes of mind;
        there are changes of heart.
There are mountains of joy one can never explain.
There are chasms of sheer, indescribable pain.
Times of sharing the last wisp of hope we possess,
Times of greed, grasping more
        so that others have less,
Lifetime hoarding of what we believe we can own,
And yet, when we leave, we must leave all alone.

SOUPY RUMINATION

I am sitting here slurping hot chowder of lobster
     From rocky New England's bleak shore.
I confess, I'm bemused that this seafaring nipper
     Could get quite this far from his home.
Were there many involved to displace this crustacean
     Who might not have wanted to roam ?
Could it be, this one soupcan contains parts and pieces of,
     Not just one creature, but more ?
Were they babies, too small for the haute cuisine crowd,
     Boiled and diced-up for lower-class meals ?
And the spuds for this chowder ; are they from New England,
     Or shipped in from Idaho fields ?
What about the milk ? Were these contented cows, roaming free,
     Proud of the burden they bore ?
And the spices ? Home-grown, or from nations abroad
     Where they force kids and don't treat 'em right ?
All these worries I fretted while scooping my soup,
     Tension building with every bite.
WOW ! I think I should get me a life !
     Is this all that I'm using my precious time for ?

PHONECALL TO MY MECHANIC

I'm reluctant to say he's forgotten me cold,
Though the notion is growing as slowly as mold,
But I'd not want him thinking I'd whimper or scold
Or that I'd hold him up if he felt buttonholed.
Still I hate to just wait till I'm senile and old.
(O, I do hope I've not "fallen out of the fold")
Well, I think he is glad when his judgment is polled
On some truck or used car that is offered or sold.
When I called on line two and he answered, he told
That insurance affairs on his line one now lolled.
He would finish that call if he might be so bold.
He said, "I'll call right back", and our lives onward rolled.

By the time he calls back, two more ships could be shoaled,
Many lifers from prison might then be paroled,
And through acres of daisies I might since have strolled !
Sure, what fine herds of cattle might wander the wold ?
What expanses and vistas might one yet behold ?
What great portents of future could one have foretold ?
Carbound cops could a million safe miles have patrolled,
Politicians their legacy would have extolled,
Used car salesmen, twelve suckers they might have cajoled,
On computer, I could through vast data have scrolled,
On a lake, for great Northerns I should now have trolled,
Were it Yuletide, eight ditties I might have caroled !

Boy, I hate to admit he's forgotten me cold !
I will exercise patience until I'm consoled
And just wait by the phone till my temper's controlled.
Up to this time his word has been valued like gold
But he sure has a timeless conception of "Hold" !

(Two days later, he "called right back".)

117

HIGH CLASS RUMPOT

I sit and sip a gentle brew to kill a little time
And, having no distractions, start to pen this little rhyme.
I think of those, alone like me, who sought the amber glass
To conjure up forgetful fog and force the time to pass
But, having stored their hunger or their problem or their pain,
Forever seek the comfort zone and do it all again.
Yet I have no intent to dull the now or hide the past
But revel in my lifetime store of friends that I hold fast.
Good friends, who shared a glass or two
        and shared their lives as well.
Who truly lived and took the time to listen and to tell.
Perhaps it is not killing time, but hoarding, jealously,
And does the liquor help or hurt in close proximity ?
And so I sit and sip and wander through my memory
To visit my old friends and kin that I alone can see.
Their voice, their smile, their quirks and habits, always crystal-clear,
But always that exquisite ache : unreachable, yet near.
Unlike the boozer's quest for brief insensibility,
I use the brew to raise the shades and light the used-to-be.

I'll have one more. A few more ghosts await and beckon me.
It's fortunate, the thing I love comes quick and nearly free.
It never was the cordials ... but the cordiality.

Few people confront a doppelganger, and that's just as well.
But when you suddenly meet someone who, time and space considerations
dictate, could not possibly be who you think
it is, and when this association lasts for more than a year, you
are left grasping for explanations.

PARTIAL RECALL

Did they clone you, Laura Ricker ?
    Were you someone else one time ?
If my brain would function quicker,
    Could I get you off my mind ?
Not a flashy prom queen beauty,
    She's attractive all the same,
But I think it's more internal :
    Same seduction, different name.
While she seems a little scattered,
    It's the million things to do ;
Not a "dresser" or a "primper'
    But a woman, through and through.
Self-possessed and sinew-tough
    While keeping up a hectic pace;
In-control, yet always worried,
    Fragile care-lines in her face.
Who became you, Laura Ricker ?
    Did I know her well one time
In a prior incarnation ?
    Was it hers, or was it mine ?
Was it here, or was it elsewhere,
    Maybe forty years ago ?
Why does every word and gesture
    Seem like someone I should know ?
Did I know her, or just wish it ?
    Did I never tell her so ?
In a time warp situation,
    What makes memory ebb and flow ?

Though I'd swear we met somewhere, sometime,
    She knows me not at all.
How could her reincarnation
    Know what only I recall ?

Should I ask her ? Should I tell her ?
        Would she laugh or cry instead ?
Is not-knowing worse than knowing ?
        Is it truth or doubt I dread ?

No, don't tell me. Let me keep her
        Vague and lovely in my mind.
When we speak our mind in silence
        Are we being cruel or kind ?
How much harm or good could issue
        Setting déjà vu aright ?
Let's remain like two ships passing
        On the ocean in the night.
Could I make a bit of difference ?
        Cheer her journey ? Share her load ?
Soften stones and move the boulders
        On that path we call life's road ?
No, I don't expect an answer :
        Just one life is all we owe.
God go with you, Laura Ricker,
        And your ghost I used to know.

*   *   *   *   *

OPPORTUNITY

When the wonders of Christmastime fill you
With the joys of the holiday milieu
And strangers' "from-the-heart" kindnesses thrill you,
When you get to reciprocate … will you ?

VOLUNTARY VISITATION

I like to go to the graveyard
      when there's no living soul around.
It's quiet and peaceful and beautiful
      when they're not puttin' someone down.
For it's carefully mowed and planted and pruned
      and cared for every day.
Too bad folks just see and enjoy it
      once a year at the end of May.
It's pretty nostalgic to walk along,
      birds singing in the trees ;
You can see where they put old friends and foes,
      and say anything you please.
But it sobers you some for you know,
      one day, there'll be your own little plot
And all your life's work will be carried on
      by somebody else ... or not.
But in summer, it's pleasant to visit the past
      and idle on your way ;
There should be lots of time for serious thought,
      after you come to stay.
It's much nicer to choose a time to be here
      than for others to decide ;
Most funerals fall on miserable days
      when you wish you had stayed inside.

CHAPTER FIVE

POETS AND PICKERS

*   *   *   *   *

The poet is a lonely individual, seeing meanings and
relationships that busy people often miss. Still,
he can't help tooting his own horn, or sharing
his insights with whoever will listen. But when
he interacts with other poets, a whole new
world of communication opens up for him.
Professional jealousies aside, performers make
the best audience.

DILEMMA

Now and then I have to wonder :
     do I really do it right ?
Does the poetry I write
       feed people's mental appetite ?
Should I tend more toward the heavy stuff
      and ease back on the light ?
Would they rather laugh or cry or think ?
       Which policy is right ?
Then I say, if they want serious,
     they'll listen to the news
Or the soap and sitcom writers
      for the topics that they choose,
Or the academic writers
     who are always so intense,
Choosing words to shock, confuse, impress...
     but seldom, to make sense.
Well, the standup comic's nastiness
     is doubtful any time
And I'm so antique,
      I still believe I ought to make it rhyme.
So, if you folks don't mind,
     let's ignore our troubles for a bit ;
We'll recharge your drooping spirits
      with our talents and our wit.
Now and then, we have to sit back,
     take a look at who we are,
Thank our friends and neighbors ...
      all those folks who helped us get this far.
And when pride outruns reality,
     we need time to "Reset".
There's no lifetime guarantee ;
      how many more chances will we get ?

GOOD INVESTMENT

He was pacing in the lobby, in a rush and quite forlorn,
      With a parcel he would clearly like to mail.
But the office would not open for a good half-hour or more
      And he needed to be elsewhere without fail.
Through the wall I heard him whining,
       with his quarters in his fist ;
      Could he leave a handful and be on his way ?
But the cleaning lady couldn't do it, helpful as she was.
      Only I was qualified to save his day.
In a show of love and brotherhood beyond the postal code,
      I peeked out the "Private" door to lend a hand
And the smile that crossed his fretful face
        was proof of his relief
      And I knew my move was something truly grand.

In his gratitude, he offered all the quarters that he had.
      Calming him was almost more than I could do.
Was this all the money that he had ? I felt a sharp concern.
      Had he saved lunch money, or gassed up "Old Blue"?

In the end, I took six quarters and it should have been enough
      For his little parcel, barely one-by-eight,
But he must have wound it tighter
        than an eight-day mantel clock .
      Let me tell you, this was concentrated weight !

So I paid out two more quarters from my personal reserve …
      One more bad debt I'll have trouble keeping track,
But the Missus says, "Don't worry.
        You just bought some peace-of-mind.
      If he still owes, then at least he won't come back !"

IF WE COULD ONLY BUY HIM OFF

This here is just a pome to make apologies to Fred
'Cause Loxi is upset with all the rhymy things I said
And she is one to straighten out those misconceptions awful
To guarantee her quotes are true, direct, exact and lawful.

Now, when I said she said it's good
       I bought some peace-of-mind,
She thought I ought to try a little harder to be kind.
And when I said she said he owes, and won't be comin' back,
She thought my sense of humor run a little bit off-track.

For while "You'll never see a bum who owes" is what she said,
She didn't mean, specifically, to say it about Fred.
She tells me,
       "Be selective where you choose to grouse and carp ;
Four years now, and I still owe Fred. I bought his Auto Harp. "

Well, I have not had one good night of sleep
       since that dark day
When I wrote up that pome and mailed the curs'ed thing away
And I would pay good money for a life at home less tense.
Just think …I stirred up this whole hornet's nest for fifty cents !

LEFT HAND COMPLIMENT

I penned a "pome" about my pop and posted to the paper.
It's possible pop's pome went "poof !", exploding into vapor.
They're busy doing other things that people want to see,
But printing all the pomes sent in is Journal policy.
The month of May was occupied with scenes of graduations.
My lines were not included ;
("time and space considerations")
Memorial Day was next with pix of patriotic fervor.
No room was left for pomes to pique the casual observer.
Next week, elections and the anniversary took place.
My verse competed with the ads and must have lost the race.
The next few weeks, the blats were small;
 no items thought-provoking,
But was my writing published ?
Really now, you must be joking.
I fear my pome has been mislaid for Lo, these many weeks.
If they don't print my stuff next time,
perhaps we should have speaks.
It's not that I expect free papers, favors, fame or cash.
Doggone, it irks me some to think my work went in the trash.
I know a few subscribers who enjoyed my other stuff.
Good Grief, the standards of that editor are really tough !
So now, each time I'm asked to do an entertainment stint,
I'm headlined as
                    "The Poet That The Journal Would Not Print".

(Published at the same time as the above was the editor's response:)

            Well, the pome about pop has been lost.
            We'll replace it, whatever the cost.
            And we learn once again
            It's the man with the pen
            Who's the wrong S.O.B. to have crossed.

(Many readers didn't realize that I also wrote the editor's response,
     just to save them time and effort.)

LIVE AND LET LIVE

Right next to where I "tie my horse"
      when I go to work each day
The Yellow Jackets built a nest about two feet away.
At work, there's just one "hitchin' post",
      so what's a guy to do ?
That "peaceful co-existence" beats a violent set-to.
Oh, I could smoke 'em out or blast 'em
      with some kind of spray
Or plug their hole in the concrete block wall, early in the day,
But, what's the point ?
      We're all in this together anyway.
We often check each other out till one of us goes away.
But neither side shows orneriness,
      though there's potential there …
Respectful neighbors in a war there's no need to declare.
And there is always some small chance
      "the other side" will win.
It's best if we can just stay calm and hold our tempers in.

My horse, of course, is not a horse,
      but just a two-wheeled bike.
It's quicker, and it saves my joints when I must "take a hike".
Unlike a horse, it has no tail
      to aggravate the bees.
All summer long, we got along as peaceful as you please.

And then September came, so sudden.
      Summertime had fled,
And on the ground around the nest,
      my neighbor bees lay dead.
Each frosty morning after that,
      more curled-up bodies lay
Among the wanton fallen leaves where raucous breezes play.

I never told a soul
      about my summer tệte-a'-tệte
For fear they'd feel an obligation to exterminate
But what a mix of feelings
      I enjoyed all summer long !
…the secret, solo savor of a lovely tune or song.
And if, as I suspect,
      another batch will hatch next spring,
I'll live once more the pure communion I'm remembering.

Some cowboys don't want to write poetry,
But they can't help themselves.

POMEBLUES

I hate it in the morning and I hate it afternoon.
I hate it in November, February, April, June.
I hate it in the country, in the suburbs, in the town.
I hate it square, triangular, elliptical or round.
I hate it with my coffee, with my beer and with my tea.
I hate it when it's foggy, dark, or clear so I can see.
I hate it in the mountains, in the foothills, on the plains.
I hate it when it's dry, or when it snows,
or when it rains.
I hate it when I'm healthy or when deep in misery.
I hate it like a louse or tick, mosquito, snake or flea.
I hate it when my fingers and my feet are keeping time.
I hate when everything I think becomes another rhyme.
I hate the "perfect line" ... before I write it, I forget.
I hate to think I didn't write my final verses yet.
I hate it, Hate It, HATE IT !
Make it stop and let me be.
There's NOTHING that I hate so bad as
WRITING POETRY !

RAW MATERIAL

I met a wise old fellow on the street the other day.
He did not hide or call the cops or hurry on his way.
I thought I'd ask the question that has puzzled me so long.
(Old characters know everything, and never lead you wrong.)
I said, "Hold up, old guy ! Have you walked past the house of Fred ?
Has he got something going ? Is he addled in the head ?
Why IS his five-ton truck completely loaded with used hay ?"
(The bum just smiled and nodded in that aggravating way.)
"Tell me : you think he'll fertilize his big new garden plot ?
…Or else, anoint his lawn in hopes the rain will make it rot ?
Perhaps he gives, handful or peck, to garden-clubber gals ?
… Or keeps it just for sale, with "freebies" only for his pals ?"
The geezer held his stupid grin and would not speak his piece.
In fact, I wondered if he'd ever heard about Fred Liese.
"You've been around awhile," I said. "You gossip, snoop and roam.
Now tell me why Fred parks his honeywagon by his home !"
Was this guy deaf ? Should I do C.P.R., tune-up or hug ?
He made me nearly frantic with that smirk upon his mug.
I kicked his shin and grabbed his cane and thumped him on his head.
I still remember each wise word the old coot finally said.
"Fred's gathering material for poems, you can be sure.
There's nothing that inspires him
        like a load of prime manure !"

Why do people attend Cowboy Poetry gatherings ?
Here's my answer, inspired by and dedicated to
Winston Mitchell of Landusky.

A POET AND PICKER APOLOGY

We come to do our verse and songs ...
      sometimes they ain't so good.
We stand up stiff and awkward,
      like our arms are made of wood.
We borrow shamelessly
      from everyone we've ever known.
We tell the stories of the lives
      much richer than our own.
We come because we have to come ...
      (as if we had a choice !)
We try to speak for everyman
      with universal voice.
We come to share the pleasure
      of a shudder, tear or smile.
We come for reassurance :
      was it really all worthwhile ?
We're here to touch a kindred soul...
      how briefly, who can tell?
Our instrument, the spoken word
      by which we weave our spell.
We have a secret need to come,
      dismissing time and miles.
Our one reward ? ...
      your sympathetic interest for awhile.
I can't pretend to speak
      for all the artists here today
(And, even if I'm right,
      they won't admit it anyway.)
Our bodies may be broke and patched
      from regular abuse.
Our memories are sketchy
      from the stretch of over-use.
We come to share the beer and noise,
      the risk and mystery.

We tell of life, the way it was,
       and who we came to be.
It's how we beg forgiveness
       for ignoring far too much …
How much we missed of sight and sound
       and smell and taste and touch..
There's not much more to offer
       with our campfire burning low.
We're glad we crossed your trail
       and shared some comfort in its glow.
Please, help yourself to any sparks
       we kindled here today.
The rest is smoke and ashes,
       our last breath will blow away.

POETS, PICKERS AND BEEF FAT

Junie always was a lady with her noble head held high.
There were certain tasks she couldn't,
      but she never failed to try.
In the car or truck she'd sit up on her blanket by the boss,
Always kind to friend or stranger ...
      never silly ... never cross.
In the evening she'd curl up, head and forelegs on his lap.
More than once they both would nod off
      in a cozy, loving nap.
Her devotion and demeanor undiminished as before,
While her body and her innards
      aren't "pup-perfect" any more.
But it's not at all surprising he'd reward his loyal pet
With the remnants of his beefsteak ...
      best darn dogfood you can get.

The October poet/picker meeting
      I was headed for
When the man with car and dog in back
      pulled up before my door.
I grabbed my warm and wooly vest
      in case the night turned coolish.
I laid it on the seat,
      since wearing too much bulk is foolish.
It was quite a lengthy meeting
      as these things can sometimes be
And I don't believe he left the room
      to let his dog run free
So she never got a chance
      to leave protective custody
Or to deal, outdoors,
      with pressing matters, necessarily.
I assume she sat cross-legged,
      or whatever doggies do
When they can not satisfy the urge
      for number-one or -two.
When it proved no longer possible
      to hold it anymore
She was forced to simply "let it go"
      on blanket, seat and floor.

When we finally adjourned,
      he let his pal out for some air.
Loading up, we sensed that "new car smell"
      would nevermore be there.
With a heart-felt sigh, he realized
      what Junie-dog had done,
Making both of us aware,
      the ride back home would not be fun.

The moon shone bright;
      the chilly night had cloud puffs floating past.
We knew deer might be on the road
      but we kept rolling fast.
Fifty miles of close, warm atmosphere's
      a challenge to describe.
Every shot of citrus aerosol
      was needed on that ride.
With the windows open,
      I was glad I'd brought my warm wool wrap
Till it, too, fell victim
      to our "indigestible mishap".
He said, "My fault.
      I knew beef fat is tricky to digest,
So check it out,
      just now I found her sitting on your vest."
Unlike some friends who would have found that ride
      too gross and "ooky",
We made it all the way back home
      and never lost one cookie.

HE'S ALL WET

At the folk music festival weekend in Butte
      on the first of a three-summer run,
Our flatpicker from Harlem made plans to attend
      to rub elbows, show off and have fun.
Due to cartrouble, it was past dog kennel hours
      when he finally pickuped to town
So the sitter was closed and he had to take Junie
      to see the events "goin' down".
There were multiple stages; it took lots of walking,
      uphill and downhill all day long
And, though Junie's a hunting dog – tall German Shorthair –
      she's no longer youthful or strong.
So it's no big surprise she would grow tired and bored
      and revert to what dogs often do
And she stuck her cold nose up a fat lady's shorts
      and created a hullabaloo.
They survived, and met old and new artists and friends
      without panic or further mishap
And he put on an impromptu tailgate concert
      with his lariat-rope guitar strap.
Sunday morning he knew, as he crawled from his tent,
      that a shower was needed post-haste
And the KOA campground provided free showers …
      a perk too important to waste.
So he lathered and scrubbed and renewed and refreshed
      and emerged feeling like a new man
And he suddenly knew, as forgetful folks do,
      this is when the old "stuff" hits the fan.
As he stood, dripping wet, he recalled with regret,
      he had brought not one towel from his home
And he knew in his heart, telling someone this part,
      would most likely end up in a poem.
So he stared at the wall … where he suddenly saw
      the dispenser for free paper towels !
With a smile on his lips, shaking off excess drips,
      he abandoned his flurry of vowels.
Yes, he pulled and he wiped, using up lots of trees,
      but it didn't cost one extra dime
And he topped off his National Folk Fest weekend,
      drying off, one square foot at a time.

CLOWNING AROUND
(a la Jeff LaBoeuf)

O ! to be a circus clown !
     To sport a painted smile or frown.
To frolic, feint and play the fool,
     Surprise and fun the only rule.
A noisy, naughty circus clown
     Who takes his tricks from town to town.
With all the joy of raising Hell,
     I wonder if it pays so well ?
And does it differ, I ask you,
     From what poets and pickers do ?

GATHERING

In case you warm with pleasure
       As you read my little book ...
In case you might have been a friend
       Whose hand I never shook ...
If, now and then, your spirit
       Thinks and feels somewhat like me,
I hope we get a chance to visit
       In Eternity.

UNFINISHED

When I recall the poems I wrote ...
       Some good, some fair, some lacking sense,
A few I should have left un-done,
       Some silly, sad, or downright dense ...
It seems to me, the only ones
       I honestly regret
Are the ones I really thought I should,
       But haven't written yet.

Printed in the United States
141128LV00002B/5/P